Better Homes and Gardens®

MICROWAVE

Recipes Made Easy

© 1982 by Meredith Corporation, Des Moines, Iowa.
All Rights Reserved. Printed in the United States of America.
First Edition. Second Printing, 1983.
Library of Congress Catalog Card Number: 81-70396
ISBN: 0-696-00845-9

On the cover: Micro-cooked recipes include *Cranberry-Sauced Pork Roast* (see recipe, page 11), *Hot Texas Stew with Dumplings* (see recipe, page 14), and *Succotash Vegetable Salad* (see recipe, page 55).

**BETTER HOMES AND GARDENS®
BOOKS**

Editor: Gerald M. Knox
Art Director: Ernest Shelton
Managing Editor: David A. Kirchner

Food and Nutrition Editor: Doris Eby
Department Head—Cook Books: Sharyl Heiken
Senior Food Editor: Elizabeth Woolever
Senior Associate Food Editors: Sandra Granseth, Rosemary C. Hutchinson
Associate Food Editors: Jill Burmeister, Julia Malloy, Linda Miller, Alethea Sparks, Marcia Stanley, Diane Yanney
Recipe Development Editor: Marion Viall
Test Kitchen Director: Sharon Stilwell
Test Kitchen Home Economists: Jean Brekke, Kay Cargill, Marilyn Cornelius, Maryellyn Krantz, Marge Steenson

Associate Art Director (Managing): Randall Yontz
Associate Art Directors (Creative): Linda Ford, Neoma Alt West
Copy and Production Editors: Nancy Nowiszewski, Lamont Olson, Mary Helen Schiltz, David A. Walsh
Assistant Art Directors: Faith Berven, Harijs Priekulis
Graphic Designers: Mike Burns, Alisann Dixon, Mike Eagleton, Lynda Haupert, Deb Miner, Lyne Neymeyer, Trish Church-Podlasek, D. Greg Thompson

Editor in Chief: Neil Kuehnl
Group Editorial Services Director: Duane L. Gregg
Executive Art Director: William J. Yates

General Manager: Fred Stines
Director of Publishing: Robert B. Nelson
Director of Retail Marketing: Jamie Martin
Director of Direct Marketing: Arthur Heydendael

Microwave Recipes Made Easy

Editor: Marcia Stanley
Copy and Production Editor: Mary Helen Schiltz
Graphic Designer: Alisann Dixon

Our seal assures you that every recipe in *Microwave Recipes Made Easy* is endorsed by the Better Homes and Gardens Test Kitchen. Each recipe is tested for family appeal, practicality, and deliciousness.

Contents

Making This Book Work For You

Some microwave cooking techniques are similar to ones you use for conventional cooking. But the others are unique to microwave cooking and must be learned—often by trial and error. The owner's manual that came with your microwave oven probably contains several basic recipes and is a good place to start learning. But *Better Homes and Gardens Microwave Recipes Made Easy* takes you one step further. It explains 64 different microwave cooking techniques, which allow you to master more than 210 delicious recipes. Plus, it presents them in easy-to-use recipe charts that give you several similar recipes for each microwave cooking technique.

For example, in one of the charts you'll learn how to make three recipes—Bran-Coated Drumsticks, Savory-Coated Drumsticks, or Corn Bread-Coated Drumsticks.

The ingredients you need to vary for each of the drumstick recipes are listed in columns in the top half of the chart.

The ingredients that remain the same for all of the drumstick recipes are listed here in the lower left portion of the chart.

And the recipe directions, which are the same for all of the drumstick recipes, appear in the lower right portion of the recipe chart.

So, if you want to make Savory-Coated Drumsticks, just follow the chart. You'll find that you need those ingredients in the second column under the heading, Savory, as well as those ingredients listed in the lower left of the chart.

That is, you'll need the 12 rich round crackers, ¼ cup grated Parmesan cheese, ½ teaspoon dried basil, 2 tablespoons butter or margarine, ½ teaspoon paprika, ¼ teaspoon salt, and the 6 chicken drumsticks.

Coated

Bran

crumbs	½ cup 40% bran flakes slightly crushed
	¼ cup chopped sunflower nuts
seasoning	⅛ teaspoon ground cinnamon

ingredients needed for all drumsticks	2 tablespoons butter *or* margarine
	½ teaspoon paprika
	¼ teaspoon salt
	6 chicken drumsticks

To help assure even cooking, arrange the chicken drumsticks on a nonmetal rack with the meaty portions toward the outside of the baking dish.

‑rumsticks

Savory	Corn Bread
‑ich round crackers, crushed (½ cup)	¾ cup cornbread stuffing mix
‑up grated Parmesan cheese	2 teaspoons sesame seed, toasted
‑easpoon dried basil, crushed	¼ teaspoon ground sage

‑ mixing bowl stir together crumbs and seasoning. In a
‑ard cup micro-cook butter or margarine, uncovered, on
‑% power (HIGH) for 30 to 50 seconds or till melted. Stir in
‑ika and salt.
‑ush drumsticks with butter mixture; roll in crumb mixture.
‑e chicken on a nonmetal rack in a 12x7½x2-inch baking
‑ arrange meatiest portions toward outside of dish. Micro-
‑, loosely covered with waxed paper, on 100% power
‑H) for 8 minutes. Rotate dish a half-turn. Micro-cook on
‑% power (HIGH) for 4 to 8 minutes more or till chicken is
‑er. Makes 3 servings.

When you're ready to prepare the drumsticks, just follow the standard recipe directions written in the lower right portion of the chart.

To make Savory-Coated Drumsticks, start by stirring together the crumbs (the rich round crackers, crushed) and the seasoning (grated Parmesan cheese and dried basil). Then micro-cook the butter or margarine till it is melted and stir in the paprika and salt.

Next, brush all of the butter mixture over the chicken drumsticks and roll the drumsticks in the crumb mixture. Then arrange the drumsticks on a nonmetal rack and micro-cook them as directed in the recipe directions

If you decide to make Bran-Coated Drumsticks or Corn Bread-Coated Drumsticks, just substitute the ingredients listed in the columns under Bran or Corn Bread for the ingredients listed under Savory. Include "Ingredients Needed For All Drumsticks" as you did for Savory-Coated Drumsticks and follow the same directions.

The how-to-do-it photograph explains preparation steps that might be unfamiliar to you.

setting	% power
HIGH	100%
MEDIUM HIGH	70%
MEDIUM	50%
MEDIUM LOW	30%
LOW	10%

If your microwave oven has more power settings than just on and off, it has variable power. Variable power means that your microwave oven can cook at different speeds, such as low, medium, high, medium-low, and medium-high.

Microwave ovens achieve lower power settings by automatically cycling energy on and off. The periods of off energy help to equalize the cooking of foods. Most newer microwave ovens have from one to nine power settings lower than high. The names and the power assigned to the settings vary; therefore, you need a way to know what power setting belongs to which name on your microwave. To solve this problem, a panel of manufacturers and consumers met to determine the most meaningful terms. The result is the standard percentages of power and terms shown in the chart on the left.

To determine how the names on your microwave oven correspond to the standard terms on the chart (and the terms used in this book), use this simple test:

In a 4-cup measure combine 1 cup of cold tap water and 8 ice cubes. Stir for 1 minute. Pour off 1 cup of water into a 1-cup measure and discard the ice cubes and remaining water. Micro-cook the water on 100% power (HIGH) until it reaches a full boil. This should take 3 to 4 minutes. Watch the water and time it carefully. Discard the hot water and let both measuring cups return to room temperature.

Repeat the procedure with fresh water and ice cubes, using the setting you wish to test. If the water takes approximately twice as long to boil, the setting is 50 percent power, and corresponds to medium. If the water boils in less than twice the time, the setting is higher than 50 percent.

Even if your oven is labeled with high, medium-high, medium, medium-low, and low, it is best to test your oven. There are some ovens where "medium" actually indicates a 70% power setting! On microwave ovens with numbered settings, the numbers correspond to the percentage of power. For example, 5 corresponds to 50% power (MEDIUM) and 1 corresponds to 10% power (LOW).

Most of the recipes in this book call for a 100% power setting (HIGH) or a 50% power setting (MEDIUM). If defrost is the only setting other than high and off on your microwave oven, test to see if defrost might actually be 50% power. Even if it is less than 50% power, you can still use it for recipes that call for 50% power. Just plan on it taking the maximum time or a little longer.

Microwave Techniques

You don't have to learn to cook all over again just to use your microwave oven. Use the cooking techniques you're already familiar with and learn just a few new techniques.

covering: Although microwave cooking is a moist cooking method and most foods will not dry out, covering is often used to help hold the steam in and cook foods faster.

stirring: Microwaves tend to penetrate the outside areas of food first and will cook foods unevenly unless you stir them.

turning: In many microwave ovens, certain areas receive more microwave energy than others. To help food get done at the same time, you can turn or rearrange large pieces.

arranging: Another technique that helps to equalize the heating is arranging. Place single items in the center of the microwave oven. Position small items in a circle around the center of the oven and rearrange them during cooking.

When you arrange foods in a baking dish, take advantage of the fact that the center of the dish will receive less energy than the outside. Position thin or delicate parts in the center of the dish and thick or less tender parts near the outside.

shielding: You can protect (or shield) delicate foods from the intense microwave energy by covering them with a sauce. Or if you can use metal in your microwave oven (see your manufacturer's directions), shield thin or delicate portions of foods with thin strips of foil.

rotating: Foods that you can't stir should be rotated by turning the dish a quarter- or half-turn. Rotating moves food to different areas of the oven and helps it cook evenly.

standing time: Most foods, whether cooked conventionally or in the microwave, continue to cook once they are removed from the oven. But in microwave cooking this is more noticeable. To compensate, large or dense foods need standing time. That means you cook the food till it is almost done, and then let it stand till it is done.

If you've been shopping for utensils lately, you've probably noticed not only more specialty dishes for microwave cooking, but also more conventional dishes that are labeled ''safe for microwave cooking.'' And you've probably wondered if any of the dishes you already own can be used in your microwave oven. To help you decide, here are some basic guidelines.

glass, china, and pottery:
Some of the most useful utensils for microwave cooking are the glass utensils and dishes that you probably already own. With a microwave oven you can measure, mix, cook, and serve in one container.

The disadvantage of glass utensils or serving dishes is that it is difficult to tell if they are microwave-safe. Before cooking in glass, check to be sure it is microwave-safe by reading the manufacturer's directions or testing the dish yourself.

To test the dish, pour 1/2 cup of cold water into a glass measure. Set it inside or beside the dish you wish to test. Micro-cook on 100% power (HIGH) for 1 minute. If the water is warm but the dish remains cool, the dish can be used for cooking. If the water is warm and the dish feels lukewarm, the dish is suitable for heating or reheating food. If the water stays cool while the dish becomes hot, do not use the dish. Also do not use a dish or plate that has a gold or silver trim or a signature on the bottom. The metal in the trim or signature may blacken or overheat the area next to it and crack the dish.

metal:
One of the most common questions microwave users have is ''Can I or can't I use metal in my microwave oven?'' Unfortunately, the answer to that question is ''that depends.'' It depends on the brand and model of microwave oven and on the amount of metal.

Most newer microwave ovens are designed to allow you to use some metal in them. (To be sure if you can, check your manufacturer's recommendation.) If you can use metal, you'll only want to use small amounts at a time. Metal reflects microwave energy, and consequently a metal pan would reflect the microwave energy away from the food.

However, the reflective properties of metal also can be used to your advantage. During defrosting, you can shield areas that defrost early. Or during cooking, small pieces of foil can be used to shield parts of food that tend to overcook.

When using metal, be careful not to use too much. The amount of metal must be in proportion to the amount of food. For example, a foil tray should be at least 2/3 to 3/4 full.

paper: Products such as paper towels, paper plates, and paper cups make easy-to-use, disposable microwave utensils. They can be used for foods that are cooked for up to 4 minutes on 100% power (HIGH). It is not recommended to use paper products for foods that heat longer.

When you're choosing paper products for use in your microwave oven, select white ones. Sometimes the colored dyes on paper products will bleed or some may even be toxic. Also be sure to use hot drink cups for heating beverages or other liquids, because even though the cup itself will not absorb microwaves, it may become hot from heat transferred from the beverage.

plastics: Most plastics, except melamine, can be used in the microwave oven. However, they do vary in the food temperatures that they can withstand. When you purchase a utensil labeled "microwave-safe" or "suitable for microwaving," read the manufacturer's directions carefully and use the dish only for the cooking and types of foods recommended.

Microwave Safety

Microwave oven manufacturers take advantage of the fact that microwave energy is reflected by metal. They use metal in the construction of an oven to keep the microwaves inside the oven and keep the energy safely away from you.

Microwave ovens are highly regulated by federal law. The law requires that ovens cannot be operated with the door open. Two independent interlock systems prevent the transmission of microwaves when the door is not securely fastened. And a monitoring system assures that the oven will not work if the interlock system fails.

Manufacturers are required to test every oven for microwave leakage before it is sold. It must meet very strict federal standards that require microwave ovens to be safe within 2 inches of the oven door. You can be sure that any oven that is safe at 2 inches will be safe at normal operating distance.

	## Oriental	## Wine	## Beer
liquid	¼ **cup soy sauce** ¼ **cup vinegar** 2 **tablespoons water**	½ **cup dry red wine** ¼ **teaspoon Kitchen Bouquet**	1 **cup beer** 2 **tablespoons cooking oil**
seasoning	2 **tablespoons honey** 1 **teaspoon ground ginger**	2 **teaspoons instant beef bouillon granules** 1 **teaspoon dried rosemary, crushed** **Dash pepper**	2 **tablespoons Worcestershire sauce** 1 **teaspoon dried thyme, crushed** ½ **teaspoon salt** **Dash pepper**

ingredients needed for all roasts	
1	**3-pound beef chuck pot roast**
4	**green onions, thinly sliced**
1	**clove garlic, minced**
¼	**cup cold water**
1	**tablespoon cornstarch**

Place the pot roast and onions in a plastic bag in the baking dish. Pour the marinade over the roast and onions and close the bag.

Trim excess fat from the pot roast. Use the tines of a large fork to pierce the meat on both sides. Place the meat and onions in a plastic bag; set in a 12x7½x2-inch baking dish. Stir together garlic, liquid, and seasoning. Pour over the meat and onions in the plastic bag. Close bag. Marinate several hours or overnight in the refrigerator, turning occasionally.

Remove meat, onions, and marinade from plastic bag; place in the baking dish. Cover with vented clear plastic wrap. Micro-cook on 100% power (HIGH) for 5 minutes. Micro-cook, covered, on 50% power (MEDIUM) for 30 minutes. Turn roast over; cover with vented clear plastic wrap. Micro-cook on 50% power (MEDIUM) for 20 minutes or till meat is tender. Remove meat from baking dish. Let meat stand covered with foil, shiny side in, for 10 minutes.

Meanwhile, skim fat from juices in baking dish. Measure 1 cup juices; return to baking dish. Stir together ¼ cup cold water and cornstarch. Stir cornstarch mixture into juices in baking dish. Micro-cook, uncovered, on 100% power (HIGH) for 4 to 6 minutes or till mixture is thickened and bubbly, stirring every minute. Micro-cook, uncovered, on 100% power (HIGH) for 2 minutes, stirring after 1 minute.

To serve, thinly slice meat. Spoon some of the thickened marinade atop meat. Pass remaining. Makes 8 servings.

Sauced Pork Roast

(Cranberry-Sauced Pork Roast pictured on cover)

	Cranberry	Chili	Orange
liquid	½ cup cranberry-orange relish ¼ cup currant jelly	⅔ cup chili sauce ¼ cup red wine vinegar	⅔ cup orange marmalade ¼ cup orange juice 2 tablespoons lemon juice
seasoning	¼ teaspoon ground cinnamon	½ teaspoon dried oregano, crushed	¼ teaspoon ground nutmeg
extra ingredient	½ cup broken pecans	1 tablespoon canned green chili peppers, rinsed, seeded, and chopped	½ cup slivered almonds

ingredients needed for all roasts	
1	3½- to 4½-pound pork loin center rib roast (bone-in)
	Whole cloves
	Curly endive (optional)
	Seedless green grapes (optional)

Score fat side of roast. Insert cloves. In a shallow baking dish with a nonmetal rack, place roast fat side down. Micro-cook, uncovered, on 100% power (HIGH) for 5 minutes. Micro-cook, uncovered, on 50% power (MEDIUM) for 25 minutes.

Turn roast over. If desired, insert a microwave meat thermometer or probe into the meatiest portion, not touching fat or bone. Micro-cook, uncovered, on 50% power (MEDIUM) for 20 to 40 minutes or till internal temperature reaches 170°. Use the microwave meat thermometer or probe or a conventional meat thermometer to test the temperature of the roast in several places to ensure even cooking. Let stand covered with foil for 10 minutes.

Combine liquid, seasoning, and extra ingredient. Micro-cook, uncovered, on 100% power (HIGH) for 1 to 1½ minutes or till heated through. Spoon some over roast; pass remaining. If desired, garnish with endive and grapes. Makes 8 servings.

To score the fat side of the roast, use a sharp knife to make diagonal ¼-inch-deep cuts about 1 inch apart.

Use a meat thermometer or a microwave meat probe to test the cooked roast in several places to ensure an internal temperature of at least 170° throughout the roast.

Pot Roast

	Family-Style	Country-Style	Italian-Style
seasoning	½ teaspoon dried basil, crushed	½ teaspoon dried marjoram, crushed	½ teaspoon sugar ½ teaspoon dried oregano, crushed
liquid	2 tablespoons cold water	1 8-ounce container dairy sour cream	1 8-ounce can tomato sauce
thickener	2 tablespoons all-purpose flour	¼ cup all-purpose flour	¼ cup all-purpose flour

ingredients needed for all pot roasts

1	3-pound beef chuck pot roast (up to 2 inches thick)
½	cup water
1	tablespoon Worcestershire sauce
1	teaspoon instant beef bouillon granules
1	clove garlic, minced
½	teaspoon salt
¼	teaspoon pepper
3	medium carrots, cut into julienne strips
3	medium potatoes, peeled and cut into 1-inch cubes
3	stalks celery, cut into 2-inch pieces
2	medium onions, quartered
1	4-ounce can mushroom stems and pieces, drained

Trim excess fat from the pot roast. In a 3-quart casserole stir together ½ cup water, Worcestershire sauce, beef bouillon granules, minced garlic, salt, pepper, and seasoning; add the pot roast. Micro-cook, covered, on 100% power (HIGH) for 5 minutes. Micro-cook, covered, on 50% power (MEDIUM) for 35 minutes. Turn the pot roast over; add carrots, potatoes, celery, and quartered onions.

Micro-cook meat and vegetables, covered, on 50% power (MEDIUM) for 25 to 40 minutes or till meat and vegetables are tender; spoon broth over vegetables once or twice during cooking. Remove meat and vegetables to a serving platter. Skim fat from broth. Stir together liquid and thickener. Stir liquid mixture and drained mushrooms into broth. Micro-cook, uncovered, on 100% power (HIGH) for 5 to 10 minutes or till thickened and bubbly, stirring every mintue. Micro-cook, uncovered, on 100% power (HIGH) for 1 minute more. Spoon some thickened broth over meat and vegetables on serving platter. Pass remaining. Makes 8 servings.

Trim the excess fat from the pot roast so that the remaining fat is an even thickness.

Stew with Dumplings

	Beef	Hot Texas	Beer
sausage	¼ pound bulk pork sausage	¼ pound bulk hot Italian sausage	¼ pound bulk pork sausage
liquid	1½ cups water	1½ cups water	1 12-ounce can (1½ cups) beer
seasoning	½ teaspoon dried thyme, crushed 1 bay leaf	1 to 2 dried red chili peppers, seeded and crumbled 1 to 2 jalapeño peppers, seeded and chopped 1 tablespoon chili powder	½ teaspoon dried basil, crushed

ingredients needed for all stews

2	medium onions, cut into eighths
¼	cup all-purpose flour
1	tablespoon instant beef bouillon granules
1	clove garlic, minced
½	teaspoon sugar
⅛	teaspoon pepper
1½	pounds boneless beef chuck, cut into ¾-inch cubes
1	8-ounce can tomato sauce
4	medium carrots, thinly sliced
3	stalks celery, sliced
½	of a small green pepper, chopped
2	cups packaged biscuit mix
⅔	cup milk
1	tablespoon dried parsley flakes
1	cup shredded cheddar cheese

To make dumplings, evenly drop batter in mounds atop the stew.

In a 3-quart casserole micro-cook sausage, covered, on 100% power (HIGH) for 4 minutes. Drain off fat. Add onion, flour, bouillon, garlic, sugar, and pepper. Stir in beef chuck, liquid, and seasoning. Micro-cook, covered, on 100% power (HIGH) for 5 minutes; stir. Micro-cook, covered, on 50% power (MEDIUM) for 20 minutes, stirring once.

Stir in tomato sauce, carrots, celery, and green pepper. Micro-cook, covered, on 50% power (MEDIUM) for 30 to 40 minutes or till meat and vegetables are tender.

Meanwhile, for dumplings, stir together biscuit mix, milk, and dried parsley flakes. Drop by rounded tablespoonfuls into 8 mounds atop the hot stew mixture. Micro-cook, uncovered, on 50% power (MEDIUM) for 10 to 12 minutes or till dumplings are set. Sprinkle shredded cheese atop. Micro-cook, uncovered, on 100% power (HIGH) for 1 to 1½ minutes or till cheese melts. Makes 8 servings.

Stuffed Round Steak

	Spinach	*Carrot*	*Potato*
vegetable	1 10-ounce package frozen chopped spinach, thawed and well-drained 2 tablespoons chopped onion	2 cups shredded carrot 2 tablespoons chopped onion	1½ cups shredded potato ¼ cup chopped onion 2 tablespoons snipped parsley
seasoning	⅓ cup grated Parmesan cheese ½ teaspoon dried marjoram, crushed	⅓ cup grated Parmesan cheese ¼ teaspoon dried thyme, crushed	½ cup shredded Swiss cheese (2 ounces) ¼ teaspoon seasoned salt Dash pepper

ingredients needed for all steaks

1	**tablespoon butter *or* margarine**
1	**slightly beaten egg**
1½	**pounds beef top round steak, cut ¾ inch thick**
1	**7½-ounce can semi-condensed savory cream of mushroom soup**
2	**teaspoons dry sherry**
½	**teaspoon Kitchen Bouquet**

For stuffing, combine butter and vegetable. Micro-cook, covered, on 100% power (HIGH) for 3 to 4 minutes or till vegetable is crisp-tender. Stir in egg and seasoning. Set aside.

Trim excess fat from round steak. Pound to ¼-inch thickness. Spread stuffing over meat. Roll up jelly-roll style, beginning with the short side. Tie with string. Place seam side up on a nonmetal rack in a shallow baking dish. Micro-cook, uncovered, on 100% power (HIGH) for 5 minutes. Micro-cook, uncovered, on 50% power (MEDIUM) for 6 minutes. Turn roll over; give dish a quarter-turn. Micro-cook, uncovered, on 50% power (MEDIUM) for 6 to 8 minutes more or till done, giving dish a half-turn once. Let stand covered with foil, shiny side in, for 10 minutes.

Meanwhile, for sauce, stir together soup, sherry, and Kitchen Bouquet. Micro-cook, uncovered, on 100% power (HIGH) for 2 to 3 minutes or till hot, stirring twice. Remove string from steak; carve. Pass sauce. Makes 6 servings.

Evenly spread the stuffing over the ¼-inch thick steak, then roll the steak up jelly-roll style, beginning with a short side.

	Barbecue-Style	Mexicali	Midwestern
liquid	½ **cup catsup** ¼ **cup water** 2 **tablespoons lemon juice**	1 **cup tomato puree**	½ **cup apple cider** 1 **tablespoon Dijon-style mustard**
seasoning	1½ **teaspoons Worcestershire sauce** ½ **teaspoon dry mustard** 1 **or 2 dashes bottled hot pepper sauce**	1 **4-ounce can green chili peppers, rinsed, seeded, and chopped** ½ **teaspoon sugar** 1 **or 2 dashes bottled hot pepper sauce**	1 **tablespoon brown sugar** 1½ **teaspoons cornstarch**
vegetable	½ **of a green pepper, finely chopped**	1 **8-ounce can whole kernel corn, drained**	————
topper	1 **small onion, thinly sliced** ½ **of a small lemon, thinly sliced**	1 **small onion, thinly sliced**	1 **medium cooking apple, cored and sliced**

ingredients needed for all pork chops	¼ **teaspoon salt**
	4 **pork chops, cut ¾ inch thick (about 1½ pounds)**

In a 2-cup measure stir together salt, liquid, seasoning, and vegetable (if indicated). Micro-cook, uncovered, on 100% power (HIGH) for 2 to 3 minutes or till mixture is boiling, stirring once. Set aside.

Trim excess fat from chops. Arrange in a 12x7½x2-inch baking dish with meatiest portions to the outside. Top chops with topper. Cover with vented clear plastic wrap. Micro-cook on 70% power (MEDIUM-HIGH) for 7 minutes, giving dish a quarter-turn every 3 minutes. Turn chops. Micro-cook, covered, on 70% power (MEDIUM-HIGH) for 7 minutes, turning dish a quarter-turn every 3 minutes. Drain off juices. Pour liquid mixture over chops. Micro-cook, covered, on 70% power (MEDIUM-HIGH) for 2 to 3 minutes or till chops are no longer pink near the bone. Makes 4 servings.

To see if the chops are done, cut the meat near the bone. If it is no longer pink, they are done.

Sauced Round Steak

	Herb	Tomato	Cheese
liquid	1 cup condensed beef broth	1 15½-ounce can meatless spaghetti sauce 2 tablespoons water	1 cup milk
thickener	2 tablespoons all-purpose flour	————	½ cup shredded *process* Swiss cheese (2 ounces) 2 tablespoons all-purpose flour
vegetable	1 4-ounce can sliced mushrooms, drained 2 green onions, thinly sliced	½ cup chopped green pepper ½ cup shredded carrot	¼ cup chopped green pepper
seasoning	½ teaspoon dried thyme, crushed	————	¼ teaspoon salt

ingredients needed for all steaks	
	1 **pound beef round steak**
	1 **tablespoon cooking oil**
	Dash pepper
	Hot cooked noodles (optional)

Cut the round steak into 4 serving-size pieces. Use a meat mallet to pound the steak till it is ¼ inch thick. Preheat a 10-inch microwave browning dish on 100% power (HIGH) for 5 minutes. Add cooking oil; swirl to coat dish. Add the steak pieces; micro-cook, uncovered, on 100% power (HIGH) for 2 minutes. Turn the steak pieces over; micro-cook, uncovered, on 100% power (HIGH) for 2 minutes more.

For sauce, stir together the liquid and thickener (if indicated). Stir in the pepper, vegetable, and seasoning (if indicated). Pour over the steak in the browning dish. Micro-cook, uncovered, on 100% power (HIGH) for 7 to 9 minutes or till the steak is tender, stirring sauce and rearranging the steak twice. Serve steak and sauce over hot cooked noodles, if desired. Makes 4 servings.

Stir-Fry with Vegetables

	Beef	Pork	Lamb
meat	¾ pound beef top round steak	1 pound pork sirloin chops	1 pound lamb leg sirloin chops
vegetable	½ of a 10-ounce package frozen cut broccoli 1 medium carrot, thinly bias-sliced	1 6-ounce package frozen pea pods 3 green onions, bias-sliced into 1-inch lengths	1 green pepper, cut into 1-inch squares 2 stalks celery, thinly bias-sliced
garnish	1 cup fresh bean sprouts	½ cup slivered almonds	½ cup pecan halves

ingredients needed for all stir-fries

3	tablespoons soy sauce
3	tablespoons dry sherry
1	teaspoon sesame oil
½	teaspoon grated gingerroot *or* ¼ teaspoon ground ginger
1	small clove garlic, minced
1	tablespoon cooking oil
⅓	cup water
2	tablespoons cold water
4	teaspoons cornstarch
½	of an 8-ounce can sliced water chestnuts, drained
	Hot cooked rice

Partially freeze meat. Thinly slice into bite-size strips. For marinade, in a mixing bowl stir together soy sauce, sherry, sesame oil, gingerroot or ground ginger, and garlic. Stir in meat. Let stand, covered, at room temperature about 20 minutes. Drain meat, reserving marinade.

Meanwhile, preheat a 10-inch microwave browning dish on 100% power (HIGH) for 5 minutes. Add cooking oil to browning dish; swirl to coat dish. Add meat; micro-cook, uncovered, on 100% power (HIGH) for 2 to 3 minutes or till meat is tender, stirring every minute. Use a slotted spoon to remove meat from browning dish; leave juices in dish. Set meat aside.

Add reserved marinade and ⅓ cup water to juices in browning dish. Stir in vegetable. Micro-cook, covered, on 100% power (HIGH) till vegetable is crisp-tender, stirring twice. (Allow 4 to 6 minutes total time for broccoli and carrots, 1 to 2 minutes total time for pea pods and onions, or 4 to 6 minutes total time for green pepper and celery.) Stir together 2 tablespoons cold water and cornstarch. Stir cornstarch mixture into vegetable mixture. Micro-cook, uncovered, on 100% power (HIGH) for 2 to 4 minutes or till mixture is thickened and bubbly, stirring every minute. Stir in cooked meat, drained water chestnuts, and garnish. Micro-cook, uncovered, on 100% power (HIGH) for 2 to 3 minutes or till heated through. Serve over hot cooked rice. Makes 4 servings.

Topped Lamb Chops

	Mushroom	Carrot	Zucchini
vegetable	1 cup sliced fresh mushrooms 1 small onion, thinly sliced and separated into rings	¾ cup shredded carrot ¼ cup sliced green onion	¾ cup shredded zucchini ¼ cup chopped onion
seasoning	¼ teaspoon dried thyme, crushed 1 small clove garlic, minced	¼ teaspoon dried marjoram, crushed	¼ teaspoon dried basil, crushed 1 small clove garlic, minced

ingredients needed for all lamb chops

1 tablespoon butter *or* margarine

1 tablespoon dry sherry

⅛ teaspoon celery salt

Dash pepper

2 4- to 5-ounce lamb leg sirloin chops, cut 1 inch thick

1 tablespoon cooking oil

For topper, in a 1-quart casserole stir together butter or margarine, sherry, celery salt, pepper, vegetable, and seasoning. Micro-cook, covered, on 100% power (HIGH) for 5 to 6 minutes or till vegetable is tender, stirring twice. Set aside.

Preheat a microwave browning dish on 100% power (HIGH) for 5 minutes. Meanwhile, evenly trim excess fat from lamb chops. Slash fat remaining on chops at 1-inch intervals. Add cooking oil to browning dish; swirl to coat dish. Place lamb chops in browning dish. Micro-cook, uncovered, on 100% power (HIGH) for 2 minutes. Turn chops. Micro-cook, uncovered, on 100% power (HIGH) for 1½ to 2 minutes more or till chops are nearly done. Drain off juices, if necessary.

Spoon topper atop chops. Micro-cook, uncovered, on 100% power (HIGH) for 30 to 60 seconds more or till chops are done and topper is heated through. Makes 2 servings.

Preheat a microwave browning dish by micro-cooking it on 100% power (HIGH) for 5 minutes.

Beef-Pepper Stir-Fry

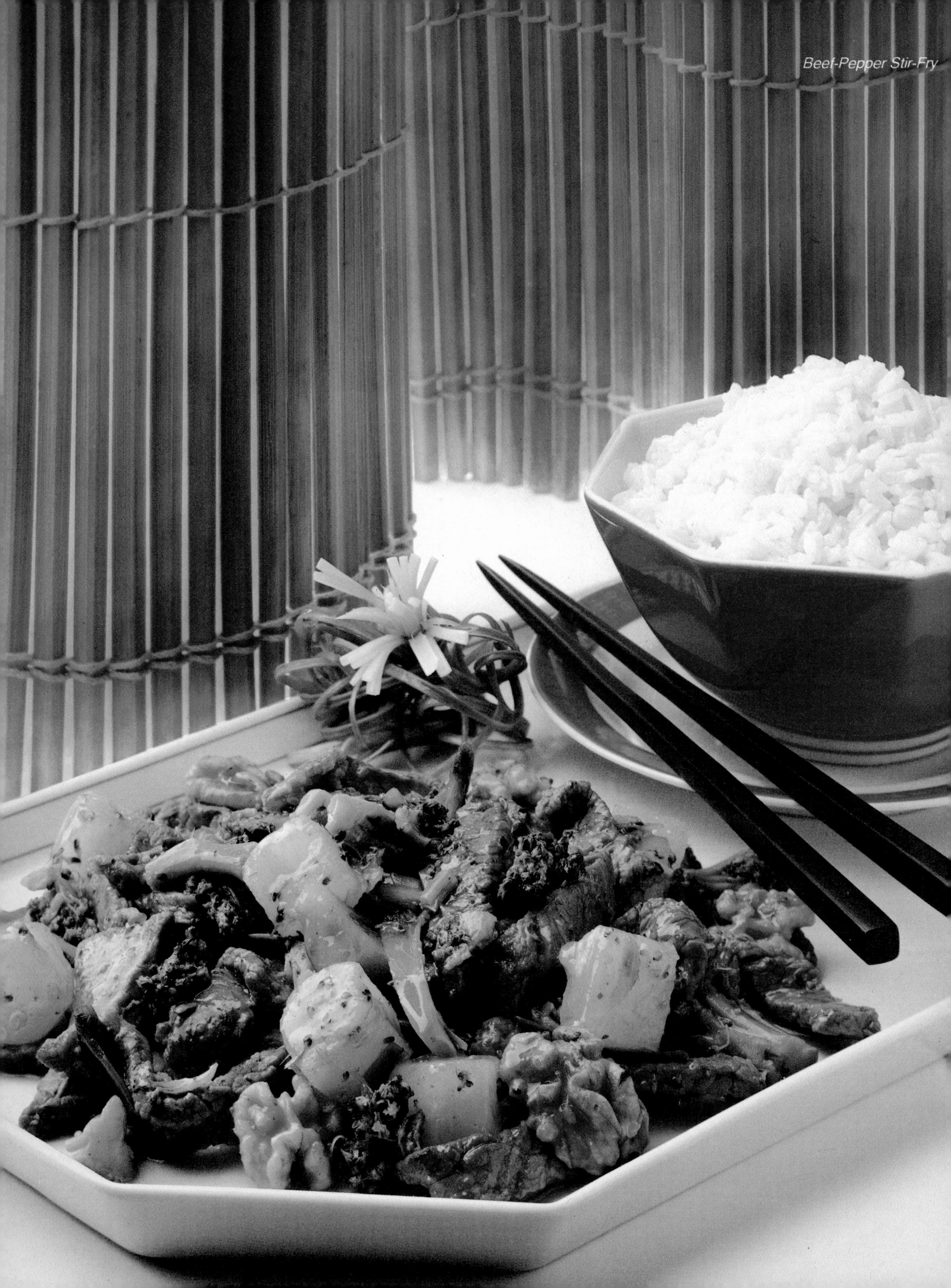

Pork

meat	1 **pound lean boneless pork**
vegetable	1 **8-ounce package frozen cut asparagus, thawed**
nuts	¾ **cup cashews**

Beef

meat	1 **pound lean boneless beef**
vegetable	1 **10-ounce package frozen cut broccoli, thawed**
nuts	¾ **cup walnut halves**

Lamb

meat	1 **pound lean boneless lamb**
vegetable	2 **cups frozen crinkle-cut sliced carrots, thawed**
nuts	¾ **cup sliced almonds**

ingredients needed for all stir-fries

1	**tablespoon cooking oil**
¼	**cup water**
3	**tablespoons soy sauce**
1	**tablespoon dry sherry**
2	**teaspoons cornstarch**
1	**teaspoon sugar**
1	**teaspoon grated gingerroot** *or* ½ **teaspoon ground ginger**
½	**teaspoon crushed red pepper**
4	**green onions, bias-sliced into 1-inch lengths**
1	**8¼-ounce can pineapple chunks, drained**
	Hot cooked rice

Partially freeze meat. Thinly slice meat into bite-size strips; set aside. Heat a 10-inch microwave browning dish on 100% power (HIGH) for 5 minutes. Add cooking oil; swirl to coat dish. Add meat. Micro-cook, uncovered, on 100% power (HIGH) for 3 to 4 minutes or till meat is done, stirring twice. Remove meat from browning dish. Drain dish.

Stir together water, soy sauce, sherry, cornstarch, sugar, gingerroot or ground ginger, and red pepper. Pour into browning dish; add green onion and vegetable. Toss till vegetable is coated with soy sauce mixture. Micro-cook, uncovered, on 100% power (HIGH) for 3 to 6 minutes or till vegetable is crisp-tender, stirring every 2 minutes. Stir in cooked meat and pineapple chunks. Micro-cook, uncovered, on 100% power (HIGH) for 1 to 3 minutes or till heated through. Stir in nuts. Serve with hot cooked rice. Makes 6 servings.

The trick to thinly slicing meat is to partially freeze it (or partially thaw frozen meat) first. Allow 45 to 60 minutes to partially freeze a 1-inch-thick piece of meat and then use a sharp knife to cut it across the grain.

Pork Spareribs

	Oriental	Apricot	Barbecue-Style
liquid	⅓ cup bottled barbecue sauce ¼ cup orange juice	¾ cup apricot nectar	⅓ cup catsup ¼ cup molasses 2 tablespoons water 2 tablespoons vinegar
thickener	1 tablespoon cornstarch	1 tablespoon cornstarch	———
seasoning	1 clove garlic, minced 2 teaspoons soy sauce	¼ cup packed brown sugar ½ teaspoon dry mustard	1 teaspoon prepared mustard 1 teaspoon Worcestershire sauce 1 clove garlic, minced
solids	1 8-ounce can pineapple chunks (juice pack), undrained 1 medium green pepper, cut into very thin strips	1 8¾-ounce can unpeeled apricot halves, drained	———

ingredients needed for all spareribs	3 **pounds meaty pork spareribs, cut into serving-size portions**
	1 **cup water**
	1 **small onion, sliced and separated into rings**
	¼ **teaspoon salt**
	Dash pepper

Trim excess fat from ribs. Arrange in a 12x7½x2-inch baking dish. Add 1 cup water and onion. Micro-cook, covered, on 100% power (HIGH) for 5 minutes. Micro-cook, covered, on 50% power (MEDIUM) for 15 minutes. Turn and rearrange ribs. Micro-cook, covered, on 50% power (MEDIUM) for 15 to 25 minutes or till tender and no longer pink. Drain off juices. Combine liquid and thickener (if indicated). Stir in salt, pepper, seasoning, and solids (if indicated). Pour over ribs. Micro-cook, uncovered, on 100% power (HIGH) for 6 to 8 minutes; spoon sauce atop after 4 minutes. Makes 4 servings.

Arrange the spareribs with edges overlapping slightly to fit in the baking dish. After partially cooking, turn the ribs and rearrange them so the least-cooked portions are exposed.

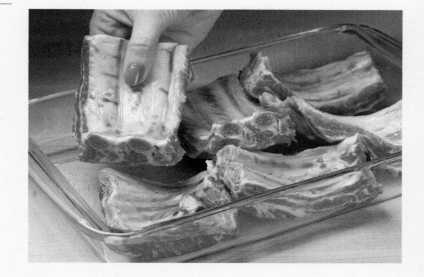

Meat Sauce

	Sloppy Joe	Spaghetti	Taco
liquid	1 10¾-ounce can condensed tomato soup 2 tablespoons water	½ cup water ¼ cup dry red wine	1 8-ounce can tomato sauce 2 tablespoons water
vegetable	¼ cup finely chopped green pepper	1 16-ounce can tomatoes, cut up 1 6-ounce can tomato paste 1 6-ounce can sliced mushrooms, drained	———
seasoning	1 tablespoon prepared mustard	2 bay leaves 1 clove garlic, minced 1 teaspoon sugar 1 teaspoon Worcestershire sauce ½ teaspoon salt ½ teaspoon chili powder ½ teaspoon dried oregano, crushed	1 clove garlic, minced 1 teaspoon chili powder 1 teaspoon Worcestershire sauce
bread or pasta	6 hamburger buns, split and toasted	Hot cooked spaghetti	12 packaged taco shells
garnish	———	Grated Parmesan cheese	Shredded cheddar cheese Chopped tomato Shredded lettuce Bottled taco sauce

ingredients needed for all meat sauces	
1	pound ground beef
1	medium onion, finely chopped (½ cup)
¼	teaspoon pepper

Crumble ground beef into a 2-quart casserole; add onion. Micro-cook, covered, on 100% power (HIGH) for 5 minutes; stir once to break up meat. Drain off fat. Stir the pepper, liquid, vegetable (if indicated), and seasoning into the cooked ground beef in the casserole. Micro-cook, covered, on 50% power (MEDIUM) for 20 minutes; uncover and micro-cook on 50% power (MEDIUM) for 10 to 12 minutes more or till of desired consistency, stirring at least once during cooking. Remove bay leaves, if present. Serve on bread or pasta. Top with garnish (if indicated). Makes 6 servings.

Pasta Pie

	Italian	Greek	Mexicali
ground meat	1 pound ground beef	1 pound ground lamb	1 pound ground pork
seasoning	1 teaspoon sugar 1 teaspoon dried oregano, crushed ½ teaspoon garlic salt	½ teaspoon ground cinnamon ⅛ teaspoon ground nutmeg	1 4-ounce can green chili peppers, rinsed, seeded, and chopped 1 teaspoon sugar ½ teaspoon ground cumin ¼ teaspoon ground coriander ¼ teaspoon garlic powder
topping	½ cup shredded mozzarella cheese (2 ounces)	½ cup crumbled feta cheese *or* shredded mozzarella cheese (2 ounces)	¾ cup corn chips, slightly crushed (optional) ½ cup shredded cheddar cheese (2 ounces)

ingredients needed for all pasta pies
1 medium onion, chopped
1 7½-ounce can tomatoes, cut up
1 6-ounce can tomato paste
1 tablespoon all-purpose flour
2 beaten eggs
3 cups hot cooked spaghetti (6 ounces uncooked)
⅓ cup grated Parmesan cheese
2 tablespoons butter *or* margarine
1 cup cream-style cottage cheese, drained

Crumble ground meat into a 2-quart casserole. Add onion; micro-cook, covered, on 100% power (HIGH) for 5 to 6 minutes, or till meat is no longer pink, stirring once to break up meat. Drain off fat. Stir in *undrained* tomatoes, tomato paste, flour, and seasoning. Micro-cook, covered, on 100% power (HIGH) for 7 to 8 minutes or till mixture is thickened and bubbly, stirring once. Set aside.

Stir together the beaten eggs, hot cooked spaghetti, Parmesan cheese, and butter or margarine. Form spaghetti mixture into a "crust" in a greased 10-inch pie plate. Cover with vented clear plastic wrap. Micro-cook spaghetti crust on 50% power (MEDIUM) for 5½ to 6½ minutes or till crust is just set, giving dish a half-turn after 3 minutes.

Spoon cottage cheese over bottom of crust. Spread meat mixture atop cottage cheese. Micro-cook, covered, on 50% power (MEDIUM) for 3 to 3½ minutes or till hot, giving dish a half-turn after 1½ minutes. Sprinkle with topping; let stand 5 minutes. Cut into wedges to serve. Makes 6 servings.

Meatloaf

	Everyday	Glazed Lamb	Orange-Glazed
ground meat	1½ pounds ground beef	1½ pounds ground lamb	¾ pound ground beef ¾ pound ground pork
liquid	¼ cup catsup	⅓ cup finely chopped chutney 1 tablespoon vinegar	2 tablespoons light corn syrup
seasoning	2 tablespoons brown sugar 1 teaspoon dry mustard	½ teaspoon finely shredded lemon peel	1 teaspoon finely shredded orange peel
garnish	Snipped parsley (optional)	Mint sprigs (optional)	Orange slices (optional)

ingredients needed for all meat loaves

2	**beaten eggs**
¾ cup	**milk**
½ cup	**fine dry bread crumbs**
¼ cup	**finely chopped onion**
2 tablespoons	**snipped parsley**
1 teaspoon	**salt**
½ teaspoon	**ground sage**
⅛ teaspoon	**pepper**

In a mixing bowl stir together beaten eggs and milk. Stir in fine dry bread crumbs, chopped onion, 2 tablespoons snipped parsley, salt, sage, and pepper. Add ground meat; mix well. Pat ground meat mixture into a 5½-cup ring mold. Unmold into a 9- or 10-inch pie plate. Loosely cover with waxed paper. Micro-cook on 100% power (HIGH) for 10 to 12 minutes or till nearly done, rotating the dish a quarter-turn every 3 minutes. Spoon off fat.

For topping, stir together liquid and seasoning. Spoon over meat loaf. Loosely cover with waxed paper. Micro-cook on 100% power (HIGH) for 2 to 3 minutes or till topping is heated through. Let stand, covered, for 5 minutes. Top with garnish, if desired. Makes 6 servings.

Carefully invert the ring mold and shake it gently to unmold the meat mixture into a pie plate.

Stuffed Cabbage Rolls

	Country-Style	Garden	Greek
breading	⅓ cup cornbread stuffing mix	2 tablespoons toasted wheat germ	2 tablespoons fine dry bread crumbs
seasoning	⅛ teaspoon dried basil, crushed	¼ cup shredded carrot ½ teaspoon Worcestershire sauce ¼ teaspoon dried marjoram, crushed	¼ cup shredded cucumber ⅛ teaspoon dried basil, crushed ⅛ teaspoon dried rosemary, crushed
meat	¼ pound bulk pork sausage ¼ pound ground pork	½ pound ground beef	½ pound ground lamb

ingredients needed for all cabbage rolls

½	cup tomato sauce
1	tablespoon water
¼	teaspoon sugar
⅛	teaspoon dried basil, crushed
⅛	teaspoon dried oregano, crushed
4	large cabbage *or* romaine leaves; *or* 8 small cabbage *or* romaine leaves
1	beaten egg
1	small onion, finely chopped
1	stalk celery, finely chopped
¼	teaspoon salt
	Dash pepper
¼	cup water

For sauce, in a nonmetal bowl stir together tomato sauce, 1 tablespoon water, sugar, basil, and oregano. Micro-cook, covered, on 100% power (HIGH) for 1½ minutes. Set aside.

Remove center vein of cabbage or romaine leaves, keeping each leaf in one piece. Place leaves in a 12x7½x2-inch baking dish. Cover with vented clear plastic wrap. Micro-cook, covered, on 100% power (HIGH) for 1 to 3 minutes or till leaves are limp.

For filling, stir together egg, chopped onion, chopped celery, salt, pepper, breading, and seasoning. Add meat; mix well. Divide meat mixture into four equal portions. Place one portion of meat mixture on each cabbage or romaine leaf. If using small leaves, overlap 2 leaves for each portion. Fold in sides. Starting at unfolded edge, roll up each leaf, making sure folded edges are included in roll.

Arrange rolls in a 12x7½x2-inch baking dish. Pour ¼ cup water over rolls. Cover with vented clear plastic wrap. Micro-cook, covered, on 100% power (HIGH) for 14 to 17 minutes, rotating the dish a half-turn after 8 minutes. Remove rolls to a serving dish. Reheat sauce, covered, on 100% power (HIGH) for 1 to 1½ minutes or till warmed through. Spoon some sauce over rolls; pass the remaining sauce. Makes 2 servings.

Turkey

⅓ cup plain croutons, crushed slightly

Dash garlic powder

½ pound ground raw turkey

Italian

2 tablespoons fine dry seasoned bread crumbs

¼ cup shredded zucchini
2 tablespoons grated Parmesan cheese
⅛ teaspoon dried oregano, crushed

½ pound ground beef

Using a sharp paring knife, cut along both sides of the large center vein of each cabbage or romaine leaf. Keep the leaf in one piece and remove the vein as shown in the photo.

Micro-cook the cabbage or romaine leaves just till they are limp and will fold easily

Fold in the sides of each leaf and roll the leaf around the meat mixture so that a packet is formed

Stuffed Burgers

	Onion	Mushroom	Olive
meat	1 pound ground beef	1 pound ground beef	1 pound ground pork
stuffing	½ cup finely chopped onion	1 4-ounce can chopped mushrooms, drained	½ cup sliced pimiento-stuffed olives
topper	4 slices Swiss cheese	4 slices mozzarella cheese	4 slices bacon, crisp-cooked, drained, and crumbled 4 slices cheddar cheese
garnish	Alfalfa sprouts	Canned French fried onions	————

ingredients needed for all burgers	
	½ cup dairy sour cream
	3 tablespoons fine dry bread crumbs
	Dash pepper
	4 hamburger buns, split

In a mixing bowl stir together dairy sour cream, fine dry bread crumbs, and pepper. Add meat; mix well. Shape meat mixture into eight ¼-inch-thick patties. Place equal amounts of stuffing on each of *four* patties. Spread stuffing to within ½ inch of the edge. Top with remaining meat patties and seal edges. Place patties in an 8x8x2-inch baking dish.

Micro-cook, uncovered, on 100% power (HIGH) for 3 minutes. Turn patties over; rotate dish a half-turn. Micro-cook, uncovered, on 100% power (HIGH) for 3 to 5 minutes or till patties are done (cook about 6 minutes for pork or till pork is well done). Drain off fat. Top patties with topper. Micro-cook, uncovered, on 100% power (HIGH) for 1 to 2 minutes more or till topper is heated through. Serve patties on split hamburger buns. Top with garnish (if indicated). Season with salt and pepper, if desired. Makes 4 servings.

To stuff a burger, spoon the filling onto the center of one thin meat patty. Top with another thin meat patty and seal the edges by pressing them together.

Oriental

1 pound ground pork

½ cup finely chopped
  water chestnuts
  Dash ground ginger

½ cup bean sprouts
  Few dashes teriyaki
  sauce

Pickle

1 pound ground beef

½ cup sweet pickle relish

4 tomato slices

Cucumber slices
Mayonnaise

*Olive-Stuffed Burgers, Oriental Stuffed Burgers,
and Mushroom-Stuffed Burgers*

Sauced Meatballs

	Barbecue	Sauerbraten	Swedish
breading	1 cup soft bread crumbs	½ cup crushed gingersnaps	1 cup soft bread crumbs
meat	1 pound ground beef	1 pound ground beef	½ pound ground beef ½ pound ground pork
liquid	1 cup hot-style catsup ½ cup water 2 tablespoons vinegar	1 8-ounce can tomato sauce 2 tablespoons vinegar 2 tablespoons water	1 cup dairy sour cream 1 cup milk
seasoning	1 teaspoon paprika ¼ teaspoon garlic powder	2 tablespoons brown sugar 1 teaspoon prepared mustard Dash pepper	1 tablespoon snipped parsley 1 teaspoon instant beef bouillon granules ¼ teaspoon ground mace *or* nutmeg
thickener	———	2 tablespoons crushed gingersnaps	2 tablespoons all-purpose flour

ingredients needed for all meatballs	
1	beaten egg
¼	cup milk
2	tablespoons chopped onion
¾	teaspoon salt

Stir together egg, ¼ cup milk, onion, salt, and breading. Add meat; mix well. Shape into 36 meatballs. Place in a 12x7½x2-inch baking dish. Micro-cook, uncovered, on 100% power (HIGH) for 5 to 9 minutes, rearranging meatballs and rotating the dish a half-turn once. Drain off fat.

Stir together liquid, seasoning, and thickener (if indicated). Pour over meatballs. Micro-cook, uncovered, on 100% power (HIGH) for 6 to 8 minutes or till the sauce becomes thickened and bubbly, stirring every minute. Serve over hot cooked noodles, if desired. Makes 6 servings.

You can shape meatballs into a uniform size by patting the meat mixture into a square on waxed paper. Then cut the meat-mixture square into even-sized cubes and roll each cube into a ball.

Cheese Casserole

	Savory Pork	Creamy Lamb	Spicy Beef
ground meat	1 pound ground pork	1 pound ground lamb	1 pound ground beef
soup	1 10¾-ounce can condensed cream of celery soup	1 10¾-ounce can condensed cream of mushroom soup	1 10¾-ounce can condensed tomato soup
cheese	1 cup shredded Swiss cheese (4 ounces)	1 cup shredded mozzarella cheese (4 ounces)	1 cup shredded Monterey Jack cheese (4 ounces)
seasoning	¼ teaspoon caraway seed	¼ teaspoon dried basil, crushed	1 teaspoon chili powder Several dashes bottled hot pepper sauce

ingredients needed for all casseroles	2 stalks celery, thinly sliced (1 cup)
	½ cup dairy sour cream
	¼ cup milk
	2 tablespoons chopped pimiento
	1 tablespoon snipped parsley
	⅛ teaspoon pepper
	2¼ cups hot cooked noodles
	1 tablespoon butter or margarine
	¾ cup soft bread crumbs
	¼ teaspoon paprika

Crumble ground meat into a 2-quart casserole; stir in thinly sliced celery. Micro-cook, covered, on 100% power (HIGH) for 5 to 6 minutes, or till the meat is no longer pink, stirring once to break up meat. Drain off fat.

Stir in sour cream, milk, chopped pimiento, snipped parsley, pepper, soup, cheese, and seasoning. Stir in noodles till well combined. Micro-cook, covered, on 100% power (HIGH) for 6 to 8 minutes or till heated through, stirring twice.

In a custard cup micro-cook butter or margarine, uncovered, on 100% power (HIGH) for 30 to 45 seconds or till melted. Stir together melted butter, bread crumbs, and paprika. Sprinkle atop meat-noodle mixture. Makes 6 servings.

Micro-cooked ground meat will become brown, but it will not become crusty like meat cooked on the range top.

Stuffed Frankfurters

	Southern-Style	Chili	Sauerkraut
liquid	½ cup water ¼ cup butter *or* margarine, melted	½ cup chili sauce	————
vegetable	————	1 cup canned chili beans, drained	1 8-ounce can sauerkraut, rinsed and drained
seasoning	————	½ teaspoon chili powder	¼ to ½ teaspoon caraway seed
stuffing	2 cups corn bread stuffing mix	1 cup cooked rice	1 cup soft rye bread crumbs
cheese	½ cup shredded cheddar cheese (2 ounces)	½ cup shredded Monterey Jack cheese (2 ounces)	½ cup shredded Swiss cheese (2 ounces)

ingredients needed for all frankfurters	
1	pound large frankfurters (6 to 8)
1	beaten egg
2	tablespoons sliced green onion

Cut frankfurters lengthwise, cutting to but not through opposite side. Place in a shallow baking dish. In a mixing bowl stir together egg; green onion; and liquid, vegetable, and seasoning (if indicated). Toss lightly with stuffing. Mound mixture in cut frankfurters. Micro-cook, covered, on 100% power (HIGH) for 4 to 8 minutes or till heated through. Sprinkle cheese atop; micro-cook, uncovered, on 100% (HIGH) for 1 to 2 minutes or till cheese is melted. Makes 3 or 4 servings.

Use a spoon to mound the stuffing mixture into each split frankfurter.

Chili-Stuffed Frankfurters and Southern-Style Stuffed Frankfurters

	Polish Sausage	**Bratwurst**	**Frankfurter**
seasoning	¼ teaspoon dried dillweed	½ teaspoon dried basil, crushed	½ teaspoon dried oregano, crushed
sausage	1 pound cooked Polish sausage, cut into ½-inch slices	1 pound cooked bratwurst, cut into ½-inch slices	1 16-ounce package frankfurters, cut into ½-inch slices
vegetable	2 cups thinly sliced zucchini	1 9-ounce package frozen French-style green beans, thawed	2 cups frozen crinkle-cut carrots, thawed
cheese	½ cup shredded Swiss cheese (2 ounces)	½ cup shredded cheddar cheese (2 ounces)	½ cup shredded mozzarella cheese (2 ounces)

ingredients needed for all casseroles

1	10¾-ounce can condensed cream of celery soup
½	cup milk
½	cup dairy sour cream
2	tablespoons chopped pimiento
1	teaspoon dried parsley flakes
½	teaspoon minced dried onion
2	cups hot cooked corkscrew macaroni

In a mixing bowl stir together soup, milk, sour cream, pimiento, parsley flakes, dried onion, and seasoning. Add macaroni, sausage, and vegetable; gently toss till well combined. Turn into a 2-quart casserole. Micro-cook, covered, on 100% power (HIGH) for 15 to 20 minutes or till heated through and vegetable is tender, stirring twice. Top with cheese. Micro-cook, uncovered, on 100% power (HIGH) for 1 to 2 minutes more or till cheese is melted. Makes 5 servings.

Top the hot casserole with shredded cheese and micro-cook for 1 to 2 minutes more or till the cheese is melted.

Herbed Chicken

	Savory	Indian	Tasty
seasoning	½ teaspoon dried marjoram, crushed ¼ teaspoon dried thyme, crushed ¼ teaspoon celery salt ⅛ teaspoon pepper	½ to 1 teaspoon curry powder ½ teaspoon salt ¼ teaspoon ground ginger ¼ teaspoon crushed red pepper	½ teaspoon dried basil, crushed ½ teaspoon ground sage ½ teaspoon salt
liquid	1 tablespoon water ¼ teaspoon Kitchen Bouquet	1 teaspoon Worcestershire sauce	1 tablespoon water ¼ teaspoon Kitchen Bouquet

ingredients needed for all chickens	
1	2½- to 3-pound broiler-fryer chicken
1	tablespoon butter *or* margarine

Wash and dry chicken. Stir together seasoning. Rub chicken surface and cavity with seasoning. Place chicken, breast side down, in a 12x7½x2-inch baking dish. In a custard cup micro-cook butter or margarine, uncovered, on 100% power (HIGH) for 30 to 50 seconds or till melted. Stir together melted butter or margarine and liquid. Brush some of the butter mixture over the chicken. Place chicken in microwave oven allowing 2 to 3 inches between chicken and oven walls and ceiling. Cover loosely with waxed paper.

Micro-cook on 100% power (HIGH) for 3 minutes. Reduce power to 50% (MEDIUM). To continue cooking allow 8 to 12 minutes per pound. Micro-cook, covered, on 50% power (MEDIUM) the first half of the cooking time. Turn chicken breast side up. Brush with remaining butter mixture. Micro-cook, covered, on 50% power (MEDIUM), for the remaining cooking time or till drumsticks move easily in the sockets and the chicken is tender, basting occasionally. Transfer chicken to a serving platter. Makes 6 servings.

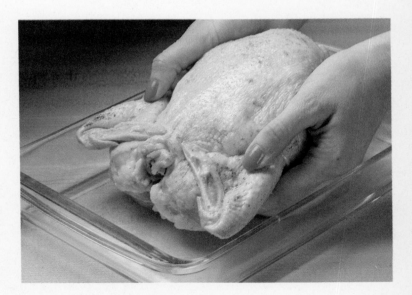

For even cooking in the micro-wave oven, start by placing the whole chicken, breast side down, in the baking dish.

Sauced Cornish Hens

	Orange	Apricot	Pineapple
liquid	1 cup orange juice	1 cup apricot nectar	1 6-ounce can (¾ cup) unsweetened pineapple juice
thickener	1 tablespoon cornstarch	2 teaspoons cornstarch	1 tablespoon cornstarch
seasoning	1 tablespoon brown sugar ⅛ teaspoon ground allspice	⅛ teaspoon ground nutmeg	1 tablespoon brown sugar ⅛ teaspoon ground cinnamon
fruit/nuts	1 11-ounce can mandarin orange sections, drained ¼ cup broken walnuts	¼ cup raisins	1 8-ounce can crushed pineapple (juice pack), undrained

ingredients needed for all cornish hens

- 1 cup chicken broth
- ⅓ cup long grain rice
- ¼ cup shredded carrot
- 2 tablespoons sliced green onion
- 2 tablespoons snipped parsley
- 2 tablespoons wild rice
- 1 tablespoon butter *or* margarine
- ⅛ teaspoon ground sage
- Dash pepper
- 2 1- to 1½-pound Cornish game hens
- 1 tablespoon butter *or* margarine
- ¼ teaspoon Kitchen Bouquet (optional)

In a 1-quart casserole combine broth, long grain rice, carrot, onion, parsley, wild rice, 1 tablespoon butter or margarine, sage, and pepper. Cover tightly. Micro-cook on 100% power (HIGH) for 5 minutes. Micro-cook, covered, on 50% power (MEDIUM) for 9 to 10 minutes more or till liquid is absorbed.

Season cavities of hens with salt. Lightly stuff hens with rice mixture. Pull neck skin, if present, to back. Twist wing tips under back, holding skin in place. Tie legs to tail.

Micro-cook 1 tablespoon butter or margarine, uncovered, on 100% power (HIGH) for 30 to 40 seconds or till melted. Stir in Kitchen Bouquet, if desired. Brush hens with some butter mixture. Place hens breast side down on a nonmetal rack in a shallow baking dish. Allow at least 2 inches of space between hens. Also allow 2 to 3 inches of space between hens and oven walls and ceiling. Loosely cover hens with waxed paper. Micro-cook on 100% power (HIGH) for 10 minutes, rotating dish a half-turn after 5 minutes.

Turn hens breast side up, arranging sides that were nearest the center toward the outside. Brush with remaining butter mixture. Loosely cover with waxed paper. Micro-cook on 100% power (HIGH) for 9 to 10 minutes or till legs move freely in the socket, rotating dish a half-turn after 5 minutes. Let stand covered with foil, shiny side in, for 10 minutes.

Meanwhile, combine liquid, thickener, and seasoning. Micro-cook, uncovered, on 100% power (HIGH) for 2½ to 3 minutes or till thickened and bubbly, stirring every minute. Stir in fruit/nuts. Micro-cook, uncovered, on 100% power (HIGH) for 1 minute more. Serve with hens. Makes 4 servings.

Coated Drumsticks

	Bran	Savory	Corn Bread
crumbs	½ cup 40% bran flakes, slightly crushed ¼ cup chopped sunflower nuts	12 rich round crackers, crushed (½ cup)	¾ cup cornbread stuffing mix
seasoning	⅛ teaspoon ground cinnamon	¼ cup grated Parmesan cheese ½ teaspoon dried basil, crushed	2 teaspoons sesame seed, toasted ¼ teaspoon ground sage

ingredients needed for all drumsticks	2 tablespoons butter *or* margarine
	½ teaspoon paprika
	¼ teaspoon salt
	6 chicken drumsticks

In a mixing bowl stir together crumbs and seasoning. In a custard cup micro-cook butter or margarine, uncovered, on 100% power (HIGH) for 30 to 50 seconds or till melted. Stir in paprika and salt.

Brush drumsticks with butter mixture; roll in crumb mixture. Place chicken on a nonmetal rack in a 12x7½x2-inch baking dish; arrange meatiest portions toward outside of dish. Micro-cook, loosely covered with waxed paper, on 100% power (HIGH) for 8 minutes. Rotate dish a half-turn. Micro-cook on 100% power (HIGH) for 4 to 8 minutes more or till chicken is tender. Makes 3 servings.

To help assure even cooking, arrange the chicken drumsticks on a nonmetal rack with the meatiest portions toward the outside of the baking dish.

Sauced Chicken

	Sweet 'n' Sour	Pineapple	Spicy Barbecue
liquid	½ cup chili sauce ¼ cup orange juice	1 8-ounce can crushed pineapple (juice pack), undrained ¼ cup chili sauce	¾ cup bottled barbecue sauce
flavoring	½ cup cranberry-orange relish	2 tablespoons brown sugar	¼ cup finely chopped onion 2 tablespoons finely chopped green pepper 2 teaspoons chili powder

ingredients needed for all chickens
1 2½- to 3-pound broiler-fryer chicken, cut up
1 tablespoon water
2 teaspoons cornstarch
Hot cooked rice (optional)

In a 12x7½x2-inch baking dish arrange chicken, skin side down, with the meatiest portions toward the outside. Loosely cover with waxed paper. Micro-cook on 100% power (HIGH) for 9 minutes, rotating the dish a half-turn after 5 minutes.

Meanwhile, stir together liquid and flavoring. Drain fat off chicken. Turn chicken pieces skin side up. Spoon liquid mixture over chicken. Loosely cover with waxed paper. Micro-cook on 100% power (HIGH) for 10 to 11 minutes or till chicken is tender, basting chicken and rotating dish a half-turn after 5 minutes. Transfer chicken to platter. Keep warm.

Skim fat from juices. Measure *1 cup* of the juices in a 2 cup measure. Stir together water and cornstarch. Stir into the reserved 1 cup juices. Micro-cook, uncovered, on 100% power (HIGH) for 2 minutes or till thickened and bubbly, stirring every minute. Micro-cook, uncovered, 2 minutes more, stirring after 1 minute. Spoon some sauce over chicken; pass remaining sauce. Serve chicken and sauce with hot cooked rice, if desired. Makes 6 servings.

Arrange the chicken pieces in the baking dish with the meatiest portions to the outside of the dish. The bony pieces, such as the wings and back, should be toward the center of the dish; the meaty pieces, such as the breast, drumsticks, and thighs, should be toward the outside.

Chicken Rolls

	Saltimbocca	Bacon-Cheddar	Kiev-Style
filling	4 thin slices fully cooked ham 4 thin slices Swiss cheese 1 small tomato, peeled, seeded, and chopped	½ cup shredded cheddar cheese (2 ounces) 4 slices bacon, crisp-cooked, drained, and crumbled	½ of a ¼-pound stick of butter, chilled and cut into four 2½-inch-long sticks 2 tablespoons finely chopped onion 2 tablespoons snipped parsley
seasoning	1½ teaspoons snipped chives	1½ teaspoons dry mustard	2 tablespoons snipped parsley Dash garlic powder
liquid	1 teaspoon lemon juice	———	2 tablespoons dry white wine

ingredients needed for all chicken rolls

- 3 tablespoons fine dry bread crumbs
- 2 teaspoons snipped parsley
- ¼ teaspoon paprika
- ⅛ teaspoon salt
- ⅛ teaspoon dried marjoram, crushed
- 2 whole large chicken breasts, skinned, boned, and halved lengthwise
- 2 tablespoons butter *or* margarine
- 1 tablespoon butter *or* margarine
- 1 tablespoon all-purpose flour
- ⅛ teaspoon salt
- Dash pepper
- ⅔ cup milk

Stir together bread crumbs, 2 teaspoons parsley, paprika, ⅛ teaspoon salt, and marjoram. Set aside. Place 1 piece of chicken, boned side up, between 2 pieces of clear plastic wrap. Working from the center to the edges, pound lightly with a meat mallet, forming a rectangle about ⅛ inch thick. Remove plastic wrap. Repeat with remaining chicken.

Place filling on each chicken breast, trimming, if necessary, to fit within ¼ inch of edges. Fold in sides; roll up jelly-roll style. Place seam side down in a shallow baking dish.

Micro-cook 2 tablespoons butter or margarine, uncovered, on 100% power (HIGH) for 30 to 45 seconds or till melted. Brush melted butter or margarine atop chicken rolls in baking dish. Sprinkle with crumb mixture. Micro-cook, uncovered, on 50% power (MEDIUM) for 15 to 20 minutes or till chicken is tender, rotating dish a half-turn every 5 minutes.

For sauce, in a 2-cup measure micro-cook 1 tablespoon butter or margarine, uncovered, on 100% power (HIGH) for 30 to 40 seconds or till melted. Stir in flour, ⅛ teaspoon salt, pepper, and seasoning. Stir in milk. Micro-cook, uncovered, on 100% power (HIGH) for 2½ to 3 minutes or till thickened and bubbly, stirring every minute. Micro-cook, uncovered, 1 minute more. Stir in liquid (if indicated). Serve over chicken rolls. Makes 4 servings.

Sauced Turkey

	Apple	Apricot	Tangy Barbecue
liquid	1 8½-ounce can applesauce ¼ cup jellied cranberry sauce Few drops red food coloring (optional)	¾ cup apricot preserves 3 tablespoons apricot nectar	½ cup bottled barbecue sauce
flavoring	⅛ teaspoon ground nutmeg	2 teaspoons lemon juice ¼ teaspoon ground cinnamon	1 orange, peeled, sectioned, and chopped
ingredients needed for all turkey roasts	1 3- to 3½-pound frozen boneless turkey roast, thawed		

Place thawed turkey roast, fat side up, on a nonmetal rack in a shallow baking dish. Micro-cook, uncovered, on 100% power (HIGH) for 20 minutes, rotating the dish a half-turn and turning the roast over after 10 minutes. Micro-cook, uncovered, on 50% power (MEDIUM) for 35 to 45 minutes or till internal temperature reaches 170°, turning roast over after 15 minutes. Let stand covered with foil, shiny side in, for 10 to 15 minutes.

Meanwhile, for sauce, in a small nonmetal mixing bowl stir together liquid and flavoring. Micro-cook, uncovered, on 100% power (HIGH) for 1½ to 2½ minutes or till sauce is heated through. Spoon some of the sauce over roast; pass the remaining sauce. Makes 12 servings.

Allow the turkey roast to stand covered with foil, shiny side in, for 10 to 15 minutes after micro-cooking. This standing time allows the roast to continue to cook, even though it is out of the microwave oven.

	Salmon	Tuna	Fish
vegetable	1 **10-ounce package frozen asparagus spears**	1 **10-ounce package frozen broccoli spears**	1 **10-ounce package frozen broccoli spears**
cheese	½ **cup shredded American cheese (2 ounces)**	½ **cup shredded *process* Gruyère cheese (2 ounces)**	½ **cup shredded *process* Swiss cheese (2 ounces)**
fish	1 **15½-ounce can salmon, drained, skin and bones removed, and broken into chunks**	1 **12½-ounce can tuna, drained and broken into chunks**	1 **pound frozen fish fillets, cooked, drained, and broken into chunks**

ingredients needed for all souffléed fish	
1	**tablespoon water**
⅔	**cup mayonnaise *or* salad dressing**
½	**teaspoon finely shredded lemon peel**
2	**egg whites**
⅛	**teaspoon cream of tartar**
	Dash salt
2	**tablespoons sliced almonds, toasted**
	Lemon wedges (optional)

Place water and vegetable in a 12x7½x2-inch baking dish. Micro-cook, covered with vented clear plastic wrap, on 100% power (HIGH) for 5 to 7 minutes, separating and rearranging vegetable once. Drain. Halve any large vegetables lengthwise. Arrange vegetable in the 12x7½x2-inch baking dish or on a nonmetal platter.

Combine mayonnaise, lemon peel, and cheese. Gently fold *half* of the mayonnaise mixture into the fish; spoon atop vegetable. Beat egg whites, cream of tartar, and salt till stiff peaks form. Fold in the remaining mayonnaise mixture.

Spoon egg white-mayonnaise mixture atop fish mixture and vegetable. Sprinkle with sliced almonds. Micro-cook, uncovered, on 50% power (MEDIUM) for 8 to 10 minutes or till egg white-mayonnaise mixture is soft-set, giving dish a quarter-turn every 3 minutes. Garnish with lemon wedges, if desired. Makes 4 servings.

Test to see if the egg white-mayonnaise mixture is soft-set by inserting a knife just off center. If the knife comes out nearly clean, the mixture is soft-set.

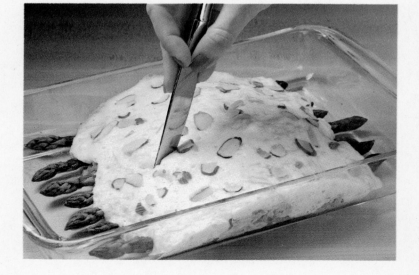

Salmon-Cheese Souffléed Vegetables

Buttered Fillets

	Lemon	Lime	Tarragon
seasoning	2 teaspoons lemon juice	2 teaspoons lime juice	¼ teaspoon dried tarragon, crushed
garnish	½ teaspoon shredded lemon peel	½ teaspoon shredded lime peel	Parsley sprigs

ingredients needed for all fillets	
1	**pound fresh *or* frozen fish fillets (about ½ inch thick)**
1	**tablespoon water**
¼	**cup butter *or* margarine**

Thaw fish, if frozen.* Arrange fillets in a 12x7½x2-inch baking dish. (If fillets vary in thickness, turn under any thin portions so total thickness is about ½ inch.) Sprinkle water over fillets. Cover with vented clear plastic wrap. Micro-cook on 100% power (HIGH) for 3 to 5 minutes or till fish flakes easily when tested with a fork, rotating the dish a half-turn after 2 minutes. Remove fish fillets to a serving platter.

In a small nonmetal bowl micro-cook butter or margarine, uncovered, on 100% power (HIGH) for 40 seconds to 1½ minutes or till melted. Stir in seasoning. Drizzle over fish fillets. Top with garnish. Makes 4 servings.

*NOTE: Thaw frozen fish fillets in the microwave oven by placing the paper package of frozen fillets in the center of the microwave oven. Micro-cook on 50% power (MEDIUM) for 3 to 5 minutes per pound. After half of the time, turn the package over and micro-cook on 50% power (MEDIUM) for the remaining time or till the fillets are pliable on the outside, but still icy in the center. Let stand for 5 minutes, then rinse well.

Fish fillets are easily thawed in the microwave oven. Just follow the directions given in the recipe note.

Basil

½ teaspoon dried basil, crushed

Green onion fans

Marjoram

¼ teaspoon dried marjoram, crushed

Lemon wedges

Dill

½ teaspoon dried dillweed

Lemon wedges

For even microwave cooking, turn under any thin portions of the fish fillets so that the total thickness is about ½ inch.

When fish is done, it will become opaque, white, and tender. To test fish for doneness, insert fork tines into the fish at a 45-degree angle. Twist the fork gently. The fish is done if it flakes easily as shown in the photo. If the fish resists flaking and still has a translucent quality, it is not done; if it is dry and mealy, it is overdone.

Stuffed Fish

	Corn Bread	Rice	Herb
bread or rice	½ cup corn bread stuffing mix	½ cup cooked long grain rice	½ cup herb-seasoned stuffing mix
vegetable	1 2-ounce can mushroom stems and pieces, drained	¼ cup finely chopped green pepper	1 small tomato, peeled and finely chopped
seasoning	½ teaspoon dried thyme, crushed	¼ teaspoon salt ¼ teaspoon dried rosemary, crushed	½ teaspoon dried basil, crushed

ingredients needed for all stuffed fish	1 1½- to 2-pound fresh *or* frozen dressed red snapper, head and tail removed
	¼ cup chopped onion
	¼ cup thinly sliced celery
	¼ cup shredded carrot
	3 tablespoons butter *or* margarine
	2 tablespoons snipped parsley
	Dash pepper
	1 tablespoon butter *or* margarine
	1 teaspoon lemon juice

Thaw fish, if frozen. For stuffing, in a 1-quart casserole combine the chopped onion, sliced celery, shredded carrot, and the 3 tablespoons butter or margarine. Micro-cook, covered, on 100% power (HIGH) for 2 to 3 minutes or till vegetables are tender, stirring once. Stir in snipped parsley, pepper, bread or rice, vegetable, and seasoning.

Place fish in a shallow baking dish. Lightly pack *half* of the stuffing into the fish cavity. Place remaining stuffing in a 10-ounce casserole; set aside. In a small dish or custard cup micro-cook 1 tablespoon butter or margarine, uncovered, on 100% power (HIGH) for 30 to 40 seconds or till melted. Stir in lemon juice. Brush fish with butter mixture.

Cover fish with vented clear plastic wrap. Micro-cook, covered, on 100% power (HIGH) for 8 to 10 minutes or till fish flakes easily when tested with a fork, rotating dish a half-turn after 5 minutes. Let fish stand, covered, while micro-cooking stuffing. Micro-cook stuffing in casserole, covered, on 100% power (HIGH) for 2 minutes or till heated through. Serve with fish. Makes 4 servings.

Lightly spoon half of the stuffing mixture into the fish cavity. Spoon the remaining half of the stuffing into a greased casserole.

Cheese Puff

	Broccoli	Carrot	Asparagus
vegetable	1 **10-ounce package frozen chopped broccoli**	1 **cup shredded carrot**	1 **8-ounce package frozen cut asparagus**
seasoning	½ **teaspoon dried basil, crushed**	½ **teaspoon dried thyme, crushed**	½ **teaspoon dried thyme, crushed**
cheese	1 **cup shredded Swiss cheese (4 ounces)**	1 **cup shredded Monterey Jack cheese (4 ounces)**	1 **cup shredded mozzarella cheese (4 ounces)**

ingredients needed for all puffs

¼	**cup butter _or_ margarine**
¼	**cup all-purpose flour**
½	**teaspoon salt**
	Dash pepper
1	**cup milk**
4	**egg yolks**
4	**egg whites**
¼	**teaspoon cream of tartar**

Prick vegetable package in several places. Place on paper toweling in microwave oven. (Or, for carrot, combine carrot and 3 tablespoons _water_. Cover with vented clear plastic wrap.) Micro-cook on 100% power (HIGH) for 4 to 6 minutes or till just tender. Drain well. Set aside.

Micro-cook butter, uncovered, on 100% power (HIGH) for 45 seconds to 1½ minutes or till melted. Stir in flour, salt, pepper, and seasoning. Stir in milk. Micro-cook, uncovered, on 100% power (HIGH) for 3 to 5 minutes or till bubbly, stirring every minute. Micro-cook, uncovered, on 100% power (HIGH) for 1 minute. Stir in cheese till melted. Stir in vegetable.

Beat egg yolks slightly. Slowly add to vegetable mixture, stirring constantly. Using clean beaters, beat egg whites and cream of tartar with an electric mixer till stiff peaks form. Gently fold into vegetable mixture.

Pour into an ungreased 8x1½-inch round baking dish. Micro-cook, uncovered, on 50% power (MEDIUM) for 14 to 18 minutes or till just set in center, rotating dish a half-turn 3 or 4 times. Serve immediately. Makes 4 (main-dish) servings.

For even distribution, stir the hot vegetable mixture constantly while adding the beaten egg yolks.

Test to see if the vegetable mixture is set by inserting a knife just off center. If it comes out clean, the mixture is set.

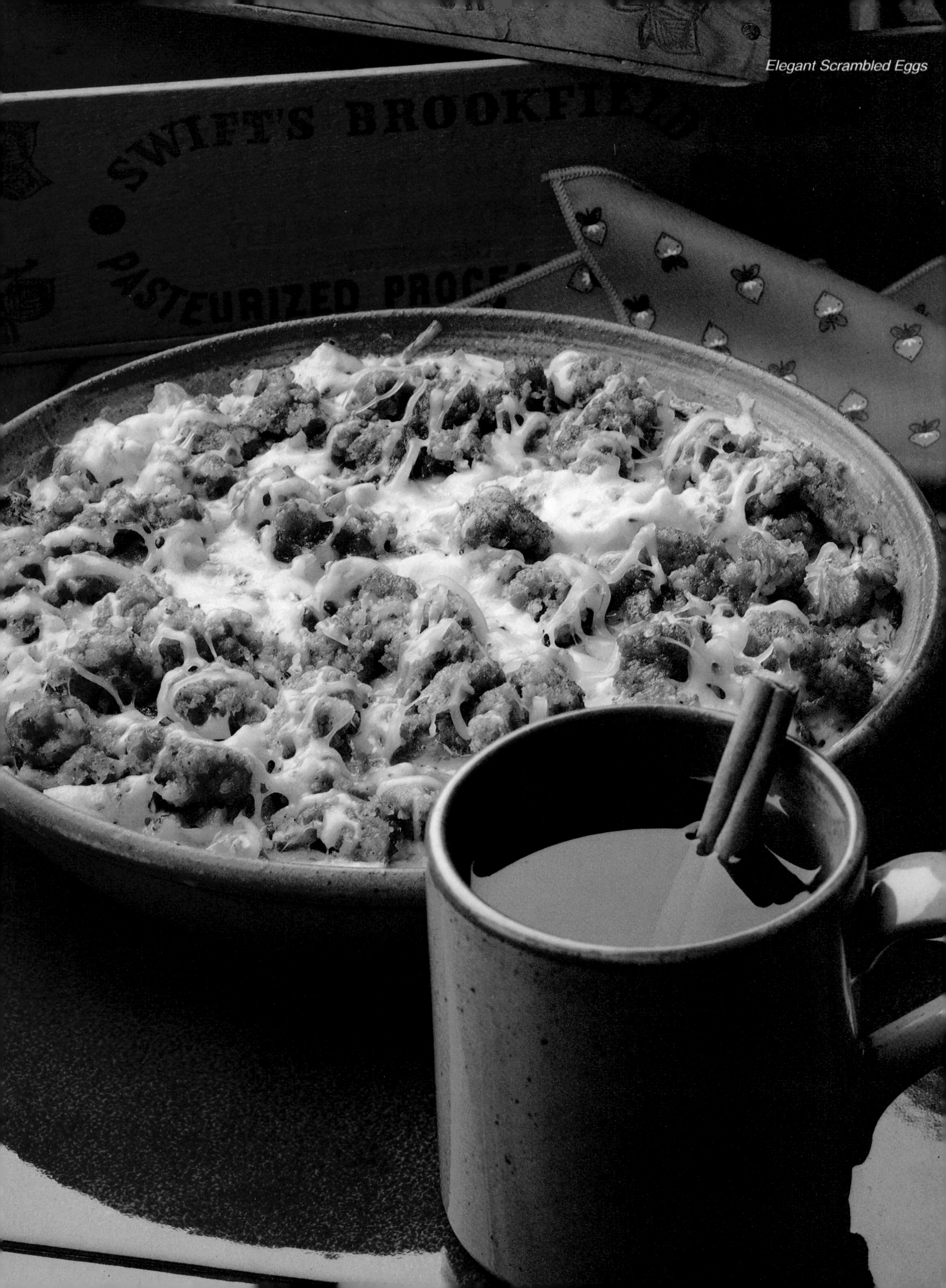

Elegant Scrambled Eggs

Scrambled Eggs

	Country-Style	Elegant	Spicy
meat	½ pound bulk pork sausage	½ pound bulk pork sausage	½ pound bulk hot-style pork sausage
vegetable	1 medium tomato, chopped	½ of a 10-ounce package frozen chopped broccoli, thawed	1 medium tomato, chopped
seasoning	½ teaspoon dried basil, crushed	½ teaspoon dry mustard	½ teaspoon dried oregano, crushed
cheese	½ cup shredded American cheese (2 ounces)	½ cup shredded Swiss cheese (2 ounces)	¼ cup shredded pepper cheese (1 ounce) ¼ cup shredded mozzarella cheese (1 ounce)

ingredients needed for all eggs	
¼	cup sliced green onion
8	beaten eggs
½	cup milk
½	teaspoon salt
¼	teaspoon pepper

In an 8x1½-inch round baking dish crumble meat. Micro-cook, uncovered, on 100% power (HIGH) for 3 to 5 minutes or till meat loses its pink color, stirring once during cooking. Drain off fat, reserving *2 tablespoons* drippings in the baking dish. Place meat on paper toweling. Micro-cook green onion, uncovered, in reserved drippings on 100% power (HIGH) for 1 to 2 minutes or till just tender.

In a mixing bowl stir together eggs, milk, salt, pepper, vegetable, and seasoning; pour over onion in baking dish. Micro-cook, uncovered, on 100% power (HIGH) for 5 to 6 minutes or till eggs are almost set, pushing cooked portions to center of dish several times during cooking. Top with cooked meat; sprinkle with cheese. Micro-cook, uncovered, on 50% power (MEDIUM) for 3 to 5 minutes or till cheese is melted. Cut into wedges to serve. Makes 6 servings.

Cheese Fondue

	Beer-Cheddar	Wine-Swiss	Swiss-Gruyère
cheese	2 cups shredded cheddar cheese (8 ounces) 2 cups shredded Monterey Jack cheese (8 ounces)	4 cups shredded Swiss cheese (16 ounces)	2 cups shredded Gruyère cheese (8 ounces) 2 cups shredded Swiss cheese (8 ounces)
seasoning	1 teaspoon caraway seed	⅛ teaspoon white pepper Dash garlic powder	½ teaspoon dry mustard Dash garlic powder
liquid	½ cup beer	¾ cup dry white wine	¾ cup dry white wine ¼ cup water ½ teaspoon Worcestershire sauce

ingredients needed for all fondues	3 tablespoons all-purpose flour
	Bread cubes *or* vegetable dippers

In a mixing bowl toss together flour, cheese, and seasoning. In a 2-quart casserole micro-cook liquid, uncovered, on 100% power (HIGH) for 1 to 1½ minutes or till hot. Add cheese mixture to hot liquid. Micro-cook, uncovered, on 50% power (MEDIUM) for 7 to 9 minutes or till cheese is melted, stirring every 2 minutes.

If desired, place in a fondue pot over low heat to keep warm or reheat, as necessary, in the casserole on 50% power (MEDIUM) for 2 to 3 minutes. Serve with bread cubes or vegetable dippers. Makes 8 servings.

In a mixing bowl or casserole toss together flour, shredded cheese, and seasoning.

	Curry	Cheddar	Mexicali
seasoning	½ teaspoon curry powder ⅛ teaspoon onion powder	¼ teaspoon dry mustard	1 tablespoon chopped canned green chili peppers ¼ teaspoon chili powder
cheese	——————	½ cup shredded cheddar cheese (2 ounces)	½ cup shredded Monterey Jack cheese (2 ounces)
topper	1 small tomato, chopped ¼ cup peanuts ¼ cup raisins	2 slices bacon, crisp-cooked, drained, and crumbled	1 small tomato, chopped 2 or 3 tortilla chips, slightly crushed

ingredients needed for all omelets

1 tablespoon butter *or* margarine
1 tablespoon all-purpose flour
Dash pepper
⅔ cup milk
4 egg whites
1 tablespoon water
¼ teaspoon salt
4 egg yolks
1 tablespoon butter *or* margarine

Micro-cook 1 tablespoon butter, uncovered, on 100% power (HIGH) for 30 to 40 seconds or till melted. Stir in flour, pepper, and seasoning. Add milk; mix well. Micro-cook, uncovered, on 100% power (HIGH) for 2 to 3 minutes or till bubbly; stir every minute. Stir in cheese (if indicated) till melted. Beat egg whites till frothy. Add water and salt; continue beating to stiff peaks. Beat yolks till thick. Fold yolks into whites.

In a 10-inch pie plate micro-cook 1 tablespoon butter, uncovered, on 100% power (HIGH) for 30 to 40 seconds or till melted; tilt dish to coat. Pour in egg mixture, spreading evenly. Micro-cook, uncovered, on 50% power (MEDIUM) for 5 to 6 minutes or till set, giving dish a quarter-turn every 1½ minutes. Reheat sauce, if necessary, on 100% power (HIGH) for 30 to 45 seconds or till hot. Slide omelet onto a serving platter; spoon sauce over. Add topper. Makes 2 servings.

To fold the yolks into the whites, use a rubber spatula to cut down through the mixture, scrape across the bottom of the bowl, and come back up and over the mixture.

Loosen the sides of the omelet from the baking dish and use a wide metal spatula to slide it out onto the plate.

Stuffed Artichokes

	Savory	Vegetable	Corn Bread
vegetable	1 cup chopped fresh mushrooms ¼ cup sliced green onions	½ cup shredded carrot 1 clove garlic, minced	¼ cup thinly sliced celery ¼ cup sliced green onions
seasoning	2 tablespoons snipped parsley ½ teaspoon dried thyme, crushed	⅛ teaspoon pepper	1 teaspoon Worcestershire sauce ⅛ teaspoon pepper
stuffing	1½ cups soft bread crumbs ¼ cup grated Parmesan cheese	1 10-ounce package frozen chopped spinach, cooked and well drained ⅓ cup shredded Swiss cheese 2 tablespoons fine dry bread crumbs	1 cup corn bread stuffing mix ¼ cup shredded cheddar cheese (1 ounce)
liquid	1 tablespoon milk	2 tablespoons milk	2 tablespoons water

ingredients needed for all artichokes	
2	medium artichokes
1	tablespoon lemon juice
¼	cup water
2	tablespoons butter *or* margarine

Cut off stems and loose outer leaves from artichokes. Cut off 1 inch from tops; snip off sharp leaf tips. Brush cut edges with lemon juice. Place artichokes and ¼ cup water in a 2-quart casserole. Cover with vented clear plastic wrap. Micro-cook on 100% power (HIGH) for 9 to 11 minutes or till just tender, rotating casserole a half-turn after 5 minutes. Remove artichokes, reserving water in casserole.

In a small nonmetal mixing bowl combine butter or margarine and vegetable. Cover with vented clear plastic wrap. Micro-cook on 100% power (HIGH) for 2 to 3 minutes or till vegetables are tender, stirring once. Stir in seasoning. Add stuffing and liquid; mix well.

Remove center leaves and choke from artichokes. Spread artichoke leaves slightly. Spoon stuffing mixture into the center of each artichoke and behind each large leaf. Return artichokes to casserole. Cover with vented clear plastic wrap. Micro-cook on 100% power (HIGH) for 2 to 3 minutes or till filling is hot and base of artichoke is fork-tender, rotating dish a half-turn every minute. Makes 2 servings.

Stuff the artichokes by spooning stuffing in the center and behind each large leaf.

Savory Soup

	Potato·Cheese	Spaghetti·Bean	Corn·Beer
first liquid	1 cup water	1 cup tomato juice 1 cup water	1 cup chicken broth
vegetable/ pasta	2 medium potatoes, peeled and chopped ½ cup shredded carrot	1 8-ounce can red kidney beans, drained 1 7½-ounce can tomatoes, cut up and undrained ½ cup chopped green pepper 2 ounces spaghetti, broken into 3-inch pieces	1 17-ounce can whole kernel corn, undrained ⅓ cup quick-cooking barley ½ cup thinly sliced carrots
seasoning	1 tablespoon instant chicken bouillon granules ½ teaspoon caraway seed	1 tablespoon instant chicken bouillon granules 1 teaspoon sugar 1 teaspoon dried basil, crushed ½ teaspoon dried oregano, crushed	½ teaspoon dry mustard
second liquid	3 cups milk	1 cup tomato juice	1½ cups chicken broth 1 cup beer
thickening ingredient	2 tablespoons cornstarch 2 tablespoons cold water	————	1 tablespoon cornstarch 1 tablespoon cold water
cheese	1 cup shredded *process* Swiss cheese (4 ounces)		1 cup shredded American cheese (4 ounces)

ingredients needed for all soups	
1	medium onion, chopped
⅛	teaspoon pepper
	Dash bottled hot pepper sauce

In a 2-quart casserole stir together onion, pepper, bottled hot pepper sauce, first liquid, vegetable/pasta, and seasoning. Micro-cook, covered, on 100% power (HIGH) for 15 to 20 minutes or till vegetable/pasta is tender, stirring once. Add second liquid; micro-cook, covered, on 100% power (HIGH) for 3 to 5 minutes or till heated through.

Stir together thickening ingredient (if indicated); add to soup mixture. Micro-cook, uncovered, on 100% power (HIGH) about 5 minutes or till mixture is slightly thickened and bubbly, stirring every minute. Micro-cook, uncovered, on 100% power (HIGH) for 2 minutes more, stirring once. Stir in cheese (if indicated). Micro-cook, uncovered, on 100% power (HIGH) for 1 to 1½ minutes. Makes 4 to 6 servings.

Vegetable Salad

(Succotash Vegetable Salad pictured on cover)

	California	Succotash	Two-Bean
frozen vegetable	1 **10-ounce package frozen cauliflower**	1 **10-ounce package frozen lima beans**	1 **9-ounce package frozen cut green beans**
canned vegetable	1 **8-ounce can cut green beans, drained**	1 **8¾-ounce can whole kernel corn, drained**	1 **16-ounce can red kidney beans, drained** 1 **4-ounce can sliced mushrooms, drained**
fresh vegetable	1 **small onion, sliced and separated into rings**	½ **of a small green pepper, thinly sliced**	1 **small onion, sliced and separated into rings**

ingredients needed for all salads	
4	**slices bacon**
2	**tablespoons sugar**
2	**tablespoons vinegar**
2	**tablespoons chopped pimiento**
½	**teaspoon salt**

Place frozen vegetable in a small casserole. Micro-cook, covered, on 100% power (HIGH) for 4 to 5 minutes or till vegetable is just tender, stirring once. (Cut up any large pieces of cauliflower.) Drain vegetable and set aside.

Cut bacon into 1-inch pieces. Place bacon in a 1½-quart casserole. Micro-cook, covered with paper toweling, on 100% power (HIGH) about 4 minutes or till crisp-cooked, stirring once. Drain off fat. Stir sugar, vinegar, pimiento, and salt into bacon. Stir in cooked frozen vegetable, canned vegetable, and fresh vegetable. Micro-cook, uncovered, on 100% power (HIGH) for 2 to 4 minutes or till heated through. Stir before serving. Makes 6 servings.

Cut the bacon into 1-inch pieces and micro-cook till it is lightly browned and crisp.

Vegetable Creole

	Okra	Green Bean	Lima Bean
vegetable	½ of a 20-ounce package frozen cut okra	1 9-ounce package frozen Italian green beans	1 10-ounce package frozen baby lima beans
seasoning	1 teaspoon Worcestershire sauce ½ teaspoon dried basil, crushed ⅛ teaspoon ground red pepper	½ teaspoon dried marjoram, crushed Dash ground red pepper	½ teaspoon dried basil, crushed ⅛ teaspoon pepper

ingredients needed for all vegetables	
¼	cup finely chopped celery
¼	cup finely chopped green pepper
2	tablespoons butter *or* margarine
1	clove garlic, minced
1	8-ounce can tomato sauce
1	4-ounce can sliced mushrooms, drained
⅛	teaspoon salt

In a 1½-quart casserole combine celery, green pepper, butter or margarine, and garlic. Micro-cook, uncovered, on 100% power (HIGH) for 2 minutes or till tender. Add vegetable. Micro-cook, covered, on 100% power (HIGH) for 2 minutes. Break vegetable apart with a fork. Stir in tomato sauce, mushrooms, salt, and seasoning. Micro-cook, covered, on 100% power (HIGH) for 6 to 8 minutes or till heated through, stirring twice. Makes 6 servings.

Frozen blocks of vegetables can be easily separated with a fork after a few minutes of micro-cooking.

Cheesy Casserole

	Broccoli	Cauliflower	Potato
vegetable	1 **10-ounce package frozen cut broccoli**	1 **8-ounce package frozen cauliflower**	2 **large potatoes, peeled and thinly sliced (2 cups)**
seasoning	¼ **teaspoon dried chervil, crushed** **Dash paprika**	¼ **teaspoon dried thyme, crushed**	¼ **teaspoon dried dillweed**
cheese	½ **cup shredded cheddar cheese (2 ounces)**	½ **cup shredded colby cheese (2 ounces)**	½ **cup shredded Swiss cheese (2 ounces)**

ingredients needed for all casseroles	
1	**tablespoon water**
1	**tablespoon butter *or* margarine**
1	**tablespoon all-purpose flour**
⅛	**teaspoon salt**
½	**cup milk *or* light cream**

In a 1-quart casserole place the water and vegetable. Micro-cook, covered, on 100% power (HIGH) for 4 to 7 minutes or till vegetable is just tender, stirring after 3 minutes. Drain off water (for cauliflower, cut up any large pieces); set vegetable aside.

For sauce, in a 2-cup measure micro-cook the butter or margarine, uncovered, on 100% power (HIGH) for 30 to 50 seconds or till melted. Stir in flour, salt, and seasoning till mixture is smooth. Stir in the milk or light cream all at once. Micro-cook, uncovered, on 100% power (HIGH) for 1½ to 2 minutes or till thickened and bubbly, stirring every minute. Micro-cook, uncovered, on 100% power (HIGH) for 1 minute more. Stir in cheese till melted.

In the 1-quart casserole stir together the vegetable and sauce. Micro-cook, uncovered, on 100% power (HIGH) for 1 to 3 minutes or till heated through. Makes 4 servings.

For the sauce, add the milk or light cream all at once to the butter-flour mixture. Stir constantly to evenly distribute the butter-flour mixture and to prevent lumping.

Vegetable Shells

	Tomato	GreenPepper	Onion
whole vegetable	4 medium tomatoes	4 small green peppers	4 medium onions, peeled
seasoning	¼ teaspoon dried thyme, crushed ⅛ teaspoon pepper	2 teaspoons finely snipped parsley ½ teaspoon dried basil, crushed	¼ teaspoon ground sage ⅛ teaspoon pepper
filling	1 cup cooked peas ¼ cup cooked rice	1 cup cooked corn ⅓ cup fine dry bread crumbs	1 cup cooked peas and carrots ¼ cup cornbread stuffing mix

ingredients needed for all vegetable shells

2 slices bacon (optional)

½ cup chopped onion

1 tablespoon butter *or* margarine

2 tablespoons grated Parmesan cheese

Parsley sprigs (optional)

Use a knife to cut off tops of whole vegetable. Hollow out the centers of each vegetable.* Place, cut side up, in an 8x8x2-inch baking dish. Sprinkle each vegetable lightly with salt. For peppers or onions, cover with vented clear plastic wrap. Micro-cook on 100% power (HIGH) till vegetable is partially cooked. Allow 1½ to 2½ minutes for peppers and allow 4 to 5 minutes for onions. Drain liquid from vegetable; set aside. *Do not* partially cook tomatoes.

If desired, place bacon slices in a 1-quart casserole. Micro-cook, covered with paper toweling, on 100% power (HIGH) for 1½ to 2 minutes or till crisp. Drain bacon; crumble and set aside. Micro-cook onion, butter or margarine, and seasoning, covered, on 100% power (HIGH) for 2 to 4 minutes or till tender. Stir in grated Parmesan cheese and filling. Spoon filling mixture into the hollowed vegetable. Micro-cook, covered, on 100% power (HIGH) for 1½ to 2½ minutes. Micro-cook, covered, on 50% power (MEDIUM) for 3 to 6 mintutes or till filling mixture is hot and whole vegetable is tender. Let stand, covered, for 1 to 3 minutes. Sprinkle with the crumbled bacon or parsley sprigs, if desired. Makes 4 servings.

*Onion centers can be used for chopped onion. Save centers of other vegetables for another use.

Rice Pilaf

	Savory	Italian	Indian
liquid	¾ cup water	½ cup water ¼ cup dry white wine	¾ cup water
seasoning	2 tablespoons snipped parsley ⅛ teaspoon dried thyme, crushed Dash pepper	⅛ teaspoon thread saffron	½ teaspoon curry powder ⅛ teaspoon ground allspice
extra ingredient	½ cup finely chopped cooked chicken *or* cooked vegetables	¼ cup grated Parmesan cheese ¼ cup sliced pitted ripe olives	½ cup raisins ¼ cup chopped peanuts

ingredients needed for all pilafs	
¼	**cup chopped onion**
¼	**cup sliced celery**
2	**tablespoons butter *or* margarine**
1	**10¾-ounce can condensed chicken broth**
1	**cup long grain rice**

In a 2-quart casserole combine chopped onion, sliced celery, and butter or margarine. Micro-cook, covered, on 100% power (HIGH) for 3 to 4 minutes or till vegetables are tender. Stir in chicken broth, rice, liquid, and seasoning. Micro-cook, covered, on 100% power (HIGH) for 4 to 6 minutes or till mixture begins to boil. Stir rice mixture.

Micro-cook, covered, on 50% power (MEDIUM) for 15 to 19 minutes or till rice is just tender. Stir in extra ingredient; micro-cook, covered, on 100% power (HIGH) for 1 to 2 minutes or till rice mixture is heated through. Let stand, covered, for 3 to 5 minutes. Makes 4 servings.

Keep the rice pilaf covered while micro-cooking. Then stir in the extra ingredient and continue to micro-cook, covered.

Grits Casserole

	Southern	Ham-Swiss	Bacon-Cheddar
seasoning	¼ teaspoon garlic salt ⅛ teaspoon cayenne	Dash onion powder	—
cheese	¾ cup shredded American cheese (3 ounces)	¾ cup shredded Swiss cheese (3 ounces)	¾ cup shredded cheddar cheese (3 ounces)
extra ingredient	—	¼ cup finely chopped, fully cooked ham	3 slices bacon, crisp-cooked, drained, and crumbled 2 tablespoons finely chopped green pepper

ingredients needed for all casseroles	
1¾	cups water
½	cup quick-cooking yellow grits
1	tablespoon butter *or* margarine
	Dash pepper
1	beaten egg

In a 1-quart casserole micro-cook water, uncovered, on 100% power (HIGH) for 4 to 6 minutes or till boiling. Stir in quick-cooking yellow grits, butter or margarine, pepper, and seasoning (if indicated). Micro-cook grits mixture, covered, on 50% power (MEDIUM) for 6 to 7 minutes or till grits are done, stirring twice.

Stir about *half* of the hot grits mixture into the beaten egg. Stir in ½ *cup* of the cheese and the extra ingredient (if indicated). Return all to the remaining grits mixture in the casserole. Mix well. Micro-cook, covered, on 50% power (MEDIUM) for 5 minutes, rotating the casserole a half-turn after 2 minutes. Top with remaining cheese. Let stand, covered, for 5 minutes. Makes 6 servings.

Stir grits into the hot water in the 1-quart casserole.

	Granola	Nutty	Bran
cereal	⅔ cup granola	⅔ cup Grape Nuts cereal	⅔ cup whole bran cereal
seasoning	¼ teaspoon ground cinnamon	¼ teaspoon ground cinnamon	½ teaspoon pumpkin pie spice
fruit	⅓ cup snipped dried apricots	⅓ cup raisins	1 small apple, cored and finely chopped
nuts	⅓ cup chopped walnuts	⅓ cup chopped pecans	⅓ cup chopped walnuts

ingredients needed for all muffins

⅓	cup water
1¼	cups all-purpose flour
⅓	cup sugar
2	teaspoons baking powder
¼	teaspoon salt
1	beaten egg
⅓	cup milk
⅓	cup cooking oil
2	tablespoons chopped walnuts *or* pecans
2	tablespoons all-purpose flour
1	tablespoon brown sugar
1	tablespoon butter *or* margarine

Micro-cook water, uncovered, on 100% power (HIGH) for 1 to 1½ minutes or till boiling. Pour over cereal. Let stand for 10 minutes. Meanwhile, in a mixing bowl stir together 1¼ cups flour, sugar, baking powder, salt, and seasoning.

Make a well in the center of the dry ingredients. Stir egg, milk, and cooking oil into the cereal mixture; add to the dry ingredients, stirring just till moistened (batter should be lumpy). Fold in fruit and nuts (if indicated). Turn batter into an airtight container. Cover and store in refrigerator up to 5 days.

To make muffins, line microwave cupcake dish or 6-ounce custard cups with paper bake cups. Without stirring batter, fill cups ⅔ full. Stir together the 2 tablespoons chopped walnuts or pecans, 2 tablespoons flour, and brown sugar. Cut in butter or margarine. Sprinkle atop muffins. Place microwave cupcake dish in microwave oven (or arrange custard cups in a circle in the microwave oven). Micro-cook, uncovered, on 100% power (HIGH) till done, rotating dish a half-turn (or rearranging custard cups) every minute. (When done, surface may still appear moist, but a wooden pick inserted into the center of the muffins should come out clean. Allow 1 to 2 minutes total time for 2 muffins, 1½ to 2½ minutes total time for 3 or 4 muffins, or 2½ to 3 minutes total time for 6 muffins.) Remove muffins from cupcake dish or custard cups. Let stand on a wire rack for 5 to 10 minutes. Serve warm. Makes 12 muffins.

Oatmeal

⅔ cup quick-cooking rolled oats

½ teaspoon finely shredded orange peel

⅛ teaspoon ground nutmeg

⅛ teaspoon ground cinnamon
Dash ground cloves

⅓ cup golden raisins

⅓ cup chopped pecans

WheatGerm

½ cup toasted wheat germ

⅛ teaspoon ground allspice

⅓ cup dried currants

Granola Cereal Muffins

Spice Muffins

	Pumpkin	Applesauce	Banana
seasoning	¼ teaspoon ground cinnamon ¼ teaspoon ground nutmeg	¼ teaspoon ground cinnamon ¼ teaspoon ground ginger	½ teaspoon finely shredded orange peel
fruit	⅓ cup canned pumpkin	⅓ cup applesauce 2 tablespoons raisins	⅓ cup mashed banana
liquid	3 tablespoons milk	2 tablespoons milk	2 tablespoons milk
nuts	2 tablespoons sunflower nuts	2 tablespoons chopped pecans	2 tablespoons chopped walnuts

ingredients needed for all muffins	
⅔	cup all-purpose flour
3	tablespoons sugar
1	teaspoon baking powder
¼	teaspoon salt
1	beaten egg yolk
2	tablespoons cooking oil
2	teaspoons sugar
¼	teaspoon ground cinnamon *or* ground nutmeg

Stir together flour, 3 tablespoons sugar, baking powder, salt, and seasoning; make a well in the center. Stir together yolk, oil, fruit, and liquid. Add to dry ingredients. Stir just till moistened (batter should be lumpy). Fold in nuts.

Line a microwave cupcake dish or six 6-ounce custard cups with paper bake cups. Fill half-full with batter. Stir together the 2 teaspoons sugar and ¼ teaspoon cinnamon or nutmeg. Sprinkle atop batter. Place cupcake dish in oven. (Or arrange custard cups in a circle in oven.) Micro-cook, uncovered, on 100% power (HIGH) for 2 to 2½ minutes or till muffins test done, rotating the dish a half-turn (or rearranging the custard cups) every minute. (When done, muffin surface may still appear moist, but a wooden pick inserted into the center of the muffins should come out clean.) Remove to a wire rack. Let stand for 5 to 10 minutes. Serve warm. Makes 6 muffins.

Add the yolk mixture to the dry ingredients, stirring just till moistened. The batter should appear lumpy; do not try to beat till the batter is smooth.

If you use custard cups, arrange them in a circle around the center of the microwave oven. Rearrange the custard cups in their circle every minute of the cooking time.

Scones

	Apricot	*Raisin*	*Date*
fruit	⅓ **cup snipped dried apricots**	⅓ **cup raisins**	⅓ **cup chopped pitted dates**
liquid	¼ **cup apricot** *or* **peach yogurt**	¼ **cup plain yogurt**	¼ **cup dairy sour cream**

ingredients needed for all scones	
1	**cup all-purpose flour**
3	**tablespoons sugar**
2	**teaspoons baking powder**
¼	**teaspoon salt**
⅓	**cup butter** *or* **margarine**
1	**cup quick-cooking rolled oats**
1	**beaten egg**
2	**teaspoons sugar**
¼	**teaspoon ground nutmeg** *or* **ground cinnamon**

In a mixing bowl stir together flour, the 3 tablespoons sugar, baking powder, and salt. Cut in butter or margarine till mixture resembles coarse crumbs. Stir in rolled oats and fruit. Stir together egg and liquid; add to dry ingredients, stirring just till moistened. Knead gently 4 or 5 strokes on a lightly floured surface. Pat dough into an 8-inch circle. Stir together the 2 teaspoons sugar and ground nutmeg or cinnamon. Sprinkle atop dough. Cut circle of dough into 12 wedges. Arrange wedges on a lightly greased 12-inch round nonmetal plate, leaving at least ½ inch space between wedges.

Micro-cook, uncovered, on 100% power (HIGH) for 3 to 4 minutes or till done, rotating the plate a half-turn after 2 minutes. (When done, surface may still appear moist, but a wooden pick inserted into the center of the scones should come out clean.) Remove scones to a wire rack; cool for 5 minutes. Serve warm. Makes 12 scones.

Place the wedges on a lightly greased 12-inch round nonmetal plate. Leave at least ½ inch of space between each wedge.

Corn Bread

	Sausage	Bacon	Ham
meat	¾ pound bulk pork sausage	8 slices bacon, cut into 1-inch pieces	¾ pound fully cooked ham, cut into ½-inch cubes
liquid	½ cup beer *or* milk	½ cup milk	½ cup apple juice
cheese	⅓ cup shredded cheddar cheese	⅓ cup shredded Monterey Jack cheese	⅓ cup shredded Swiss cheese

ingredients needed for all corn bread	
	Cooking oil (if needed)
	¾ **cup all-purpose flour**
	¾ **cup yellow cornmeal**
	2 **tablespoons sugar**
	1 **tablespoon baking powder**
	½ **teaspoon salt**
	2 **beaten eggs**

Place meat in an 8x1½-inch round baking dish. Stir, if necessary, to separate into pieces. Micro-cook, uncovered, on 100% power (HIGH) for 2 to 5 minutes or till meat is done (for ham, cook till meat is heated through), stirring after half of the cooking time. Drain off fat, reserving ⅓ cup (if ⅓ cup fat is not available, add cooking oil to any available fat to equal ⅓ cup). Remove *half* of the meat and set aside.

In a mixing bowl stir together flour, cornmeal, sugar, baking powder, and salt. Combine eggs, liquid, and reserved ⅓ cup fat. Stir into flour mixture just till smooth (*do not* overbeat). Pour batter over the half of the meat remaining in the baking dish. Sprinkle reserved meat atop.

Place baking dish on an inverted nonmetal saucer in microwave oven. Micro-cook, uncovered, on 50% power (MEDIUM) for 6 minutes, rotating the baking dish a half-turn after 3 minutes. Micro-cook, uncovered, on 100% (HIGH) for 2 to 3 minutes or till corn bread is done. Sprinkle cheese atop. Let stand for 10 minutes. Cut into wedges to serve. Makes 8 (side-dish) servings.

Reserve half of the cooked meat and sprinkle it atop the corn bread batter before micro-cooking.

Nut Bread

	Pumpkin	Carrot	Zucchini
spice	1 teaspoon ground cinnamon ¼ teaspoon ground nutmeg	½ teaspoon ground ginger	1 teaspoon ground cinnamon ⅛ teaspoon ground cloves
flavoring	1 cup canned pumpkin	1½ cups finely shredded carrot	1½ cups finely shredded zucchini
nuts	½ cup broken pecans	½ cup broken walnuts	½ cup broken walnuts

ingredients needed for all nut breads

Toasted wheat germ
1 **cup all-purpose flour**
2½ **teaspoons baking powder**
½ **teaspoon baking soda**
½ **teaspoon salt**
2 **beaten eggs**
¾ **cup packed brown sugar**
½ **cup raisins**
⅓ **cup cooking oil**

Grease a 9x5x3-inch loaf dish. Sprinkle dish with toasted wheat germ. Set aside. In a large mixing bowl stir together flour, baking powder, soda, salt, and spice. In a medium mixing bowl stir together beaten eggs, brown sugar, raisins, cooking oil, and flavoring. Add egg mixture to flour mixture, stirring till just combined (batter should be lumpy). Fold in nuts. Turn batter into prepared dish.

Place dish on an inverted nonmetal saucer in the center of the microwave oven. Micro-cook, uncovered, on 50% power (MEDIUM) for 9 minutes, rotating dish a quarter-turn every 3 minutes. Micro-cook, uncovered, on 100% power (HIGH) for 2 to 3 minutes more or till bread tests done. (When done, bread surface may still appear moist, but a wooden pick inserted into the center of the loaf should come out clean.) Let stand 5 minutes. Remove from dish. Cool. Makes one loaf.

To help prevent the nut bread from sticking to the baking dish, sprinkle the greased baking dish with toasted wheat germ before spooning in the batter.

To help evenly cook the nut bread, place the baking dish on an inverted saucer in the center of the microwave oven.

Swirl Bread

	Apricot	**Raisin**	**Spicy**
filling	1 cup dried apricots, snipped and plumped (see tip, page 93)	1 cup raisins *or* dried currants, plumped (see tip, page 93)	½ cup sugar 1 teaspoon ground cinnamon ½ teaspoon ground nutmeg ⅛ teaspoon ground cloves
flavoring	4 teaspoons apricot brandy	¼ teaspoon vanilla	¼ teaspoon vanilla

ingredients needed for all breads
2 tablespoons cold *stick* margarine
6¾ to 7¼ cups all-purpose flour
2 packages active dry yeast
2 cups milk
¼ cup sugar
¼ cup butter *or* margarine, cut up
2 teaspoons salt
3 eggs
Milk
1 cup sifted powdered sugar
Milk

Before you begin, test microwave oven to determine if it may be used for raising bread dough. To test, place the 2 tablespoons cold stick margarine in a custard cup in the center of the microwave oven. Micro-cook margarine, uncovered, on 10% power (LOW) for 4 minutes. If margarine is completely melted in *less* than 4 minutes, you will be *unable* to satisfactorily proof (raise) bread in your microwave oven.

Combine *3 cups* of the flour and yeast. Combine milk, ¼ cup sugar, ¼ cup butter or margarine, and salt. Micro-cook, uncovered, on 100% power (HIGH) for 2 to 3 minutes or till just warm (115° to 120°) and butter is almost melted.

Add milk mixture and eggs to flour mixture. Beat with electric mixer on low speed for ½ minute. Beat 3 minutes at high speed. Stir in as much of the remaining flour as you can. Turn out onto a lightly floured surface. Knead in enough remaining flour to make a moderately stiff dough that is smooth and elastic (6 to 8 minutes total). Shape into a ball. Place in a lightly greased nonmetal bowl; turn once.

Meanwhile, fill a 4-cup measure with 3 cups *water*. Micro-cook, uncovered, on 100% power (HIGH) for 4 to 6 minutes or till boiling. Set to side in oven. Place dough beside water; cover loosely with waxed paper. Micro-cook on 10% power (LOW) for 16 to 20 minutes or till dough doubles in size.

Punch down; divide in half. Cover; let rest 10 minutes. Roll each half into a 15x8-inch rectangle. Brush with milk. Sprinkle *half* of the filling over *each* rectangle. Beginning with narrow end, roll up jelly-roll style; seal edge and ends. Place seam side down in two greased 9x5x3-inch loaf dishes.

Micro-cook the 3 cups water, uncovered, on 100% power (HIGH) for 4 to 6 minutes or till boiling again. Set to one side in oven. Place loaves beside water; cover loosely with waxed paper. Micro-cook on 10% power (LOW) for 6 to 8 minutes or till dough nearly doubles in size.

Bake in a *conventional* oven at 375° for 35 to 40 minutes or till done. Cover with foil the last 15 minutes. Remove from pans. Stir together powdered sugar and flavoring; add enough milk to make of drizzling consistency. Drizzle atop warm loaves. Makes 2 loaves.

Lemon

½ cup sugar
2 teaspoons finely shredded lemon peel

1 tablespoon lemon juice

Orange

½ cup sugar
2 teaspoons finely shredded orange peel

1 tablespoon orange juice

Spicy Swirl Bread

Yeast Bread

	White	**Whole Wheat**	**Rye**
variety flour	2½ cups all-purpose flour	2½ cups whole wheat flour	2½ cups rye flour *or* pumpernickel rye flour
sweetener	2 tablespoons sugar	¼ cup honey	2 tablespoons sugar
flavoring	————	————	1 tablespoon caraway seed

ingredients needed for all bread
2 tablespoons cold stick margarine
2 packages active dry yeast
2¼ cups milk
1 tablespoon shortening
2 teaspoons salt
2¾ to 3½ cups all-purpose flour

Before you begin, test microwave oven to determine if it may be used for raising bread dough. To test, place 2 tablespoons cold stick margarine in a custard cup in the center of the microwave oven. Micro-cook margarine, uncovered, on 10% power (LOW) for 4 minutes. If margarine is completely melted in *less* than 4 minutes, you will be *unable* to satisfactorily proof (raise) bread in your microwave oven.

Combine the yeast and the 2½ cups variety flour. Combine the milk, shortening, salt, sweetener, and flavoring (if indicated). Micro-cook, uncovered, on 100% power (HIGH) for 2 to 3 minutes or just till warm (115° to 120°) and shortening is almost melted. (Temperature probe may be used to determine final milk mixture temperature of 115° to 120°.)

Add milk mixture to variety flour mixture. Beat with electric mixer at low speed for ½ minute, scraping sides of bowl constantly. Beat 3 minutes at high speed. Stir in as much of the 2¾ to 3½ cups all-purpose flour as you can mix in with a spoon. Turn out onto a lightly floured surface. Knead in enough remaining all-purpose flour to make a moderately stiff dough that is smooth and elastic (6 to 8 minutes total). Shape into a ball. Place in a lightly greased nonmetal bowl; turn once to grease surface.

Meanwhile, fill a 4-cup measure with 3 cups *water*. Micro-cook, uncovered, on 100% power (HIGH) for 6 to 8 minutes or till boiling. Set water to one side in oven. Place bowl of dough beside water in oven; cover dough loosely with waxed paper. Micro-cook on 10% power (LOW) for 14 to 16 minutes or till dough doubles in size.

Punch dough down; divide in half. Cover; let rest 10 minutes. Shape *each half* into a loaf. Place in lightly greased 8x4x2-inch loaf dishes. In the 4-cup measure micro-cook the 3 cups water, uncovered, on 100% power (HIGH) for 4 to 5 minutes or till boiling again. Set to one side in oven.

Place loaves of dough beside water in oven; cover loaves loosely with waxed paper. Micro-cook on 10% power (LOW) for 6 to 8 minutes or till dough nearly doubles in size. Bake in a *conventional* oven at 375° for 35 minutes or till done. Cover with foil, if necessary, to prevent overbrowning. Remove from pans; cool on a wire rack. Makes 2 loaves.

Brownie Pudding Cake

	## Cherry	## Apple	## Rum-Raisin
pie filling	1 **21-ounce can cherry pie filling**	1 **20-ounce can apple pie filling**	1 **22-ounce can raisin pie filling**
flavoring	½ **teaspoon vanilla**	½ **teaspoon ground cinnamon** ½ **teaspoon vanilla**	¼ **teaspoon rum extract**
nuts	⅓ **cup chopped walnuts**	⅓ **cup chopped walnuts**	⅓ **cup slivered almonds**

ingredients needed for all cakes	
2	**tablespoons butter *or* margarine**
½	**cup water**
1	**tablespoon lemon juice**
¼	**cup butter *or* margarine**
1	**cup sugar**
2	**egg yolks**
2	**squares (2 ounces) unsweetened chocolate**
½	**cup milk**
1	**cup all-purpose flour**
½	**teaspoon baking powder**
½	**teaspoon salt**
2	**egg whites**

Note: You *cannot* successfully cook any of the Brownie Pudding Cakes in a microwave oven with a turntable.

In a 12x7½x2-inch baking dish micro-cook the 2 tablespoons butter or margarine, uncovered, on 100% power (HIGH) for 30 to 40 seconds or till melted; stir in water, lemon juice, and pie filling.

In a large mixer bowl beat the ¼ cup butter or margarine for 30 seconds. Add sugar; beat till well combined. Add egg yolks and flavoring; beat till fluffy. In a custard cup micro-cook chocolate, uncovered, on 100% power (HIGH) for 1 to 2 minutes or till melted. Cool. Stir melted chocolate and milk into butter-sugar mixture. Stir together flour, baking powder, and salt. Add to chocolate mixture; mix well.

Using clean beaters, in a small mixer bowl beat egg whites with an electric mixer till stiff peaks form. Fold egg whites and nuts into chocolate mixture. Spoon over pie filling mixture. Micro-cook, uncovered, on 100% power (HIGH) for 12 to 17 minutes or till done, rotating the dish a half-turn every 5 minutes. Serve warm. Makes 8 servings.

Use a spoon to carefully dollop the chocolate cake batter atop the fruit mixture in the baking dish.

	Pecan	Walnut	Granola
flavoring	½ teaspoon ground cinnamon ¼ teaspoon ground nutmeg	½ teaspoon finely shredded orange peel	¼ teaspoon ground allspice
liquid	⅓ cup milk	⅓ cup orange juice	⅓ cup buttermilk
topping	½ cup coconut ½ cup broken pecans	½ cup broken walnuts ¼ cup regular rolled oats	½ cup granola ¼ cup raisins

ingredients needed for all cakes
¾ cup all-purpose flour
⅔ cup sugar
½ teaspoon baking powder
½ teaspoon salt
2 eggs
⅓ cup shortening
⅓ cup packed brown sugar
2 teaspoons cornstarch
⅓ cup evaporated milk
2 tablespoons butter or margarine

Stir together the flour, sugar, baking powder, salt, and flavoring. Add the eggs, shortening, and liquid. Beat with an electric mixer on low speed till combined; beat for 2 minutes on medium speed, scraping the sides of the bowl occasionally. Turn batter into a greased 8x1½-inch round baking dish. Micro-cook, uncovered, on 50% power (MEDIUM) for 9 to 10 minutes or till the cake tests almost done, giving the dish a quarter-turn every 3 minutes. Micro-cook, uncovered, on 100% power (HIGH) for 1 to 1½ minutes more or till cake tests done. (When done, cake surface may still appear moist, but a wooden pick inserted into the center of the cake should come out clean.) Let cake stand, uncovered, for 5 minutes.

Meanwhile, in a small nonmetal mixing bowl stir together brown sugar and cornstarch. Stir in the evaporated milk and butter or margarine. Micro-cook, uncovered, on 100% power (HIGH) for 1½ to 2 minutes or till mixture is thickened and bubbly, stirring every 30 seconds. Stir in topping; spread over top of cake. Serve warm. Makes one 8-inch cake.

When the cake is done, the surface may still appear moist, but a wooden pick inserted into the center should come out clean.

Spiced Compote

	Cherry-Orange	Apple-Apricot	Mixed Fruit
liquid	1 cup water 3 tablespoons Galliano	⅓ cup dry white wine ⅓ cup orange juice ¼ cup water	¾ cup peach nectar 3 tablespoons brandy
seasoning	1 teaspoon finely shredded orange peel	¼ teaspoon finely shredded lemon peel ⅛ teaspoon ground cinnamon Dash ground nutmeg	⅛ teaspoon ground cinnamon Dash ground cloves
fruit	1 medium orange, peeled and sliced *or* sectioned 1 16-ounce can pitted dark sweet cherries, drained	1 medium apple, cored and sliced 1 8¾-ounce can unpeeled apricot halves, drained	1 17-ounce can fruit for salads, drained

ingredients needed for all fruit compotes	
¼	cup sugar
1	15¼-ounce can pineapple chunks, drained
2	oranges, peeled and sliced *or* sectioned
	Dairy sour cream (optional)
	Ground cinnamon (optional)
	Mint sprigs (optional)

In a 1½-quart casserole stir together sugar, liquid, and seasoning. Micro-cook, uncovered, on 100% power (HIGH) for 1½ to 2½ minutes or till mixture just starts to boil. Stir in pineapple chunks, the 2 oranges, and fruit. Micro-cook, uncovered, on 100% power (HIGH) for 3 minutes more or till hot. Serve warm or chilled. Top with sour cream, cinnamon, or mint sprigs, if desired. Makes 6 servings.

To slice an orange, start by removing the peel and cutting away all of the white membrane. Then use a serrated knife or a paring knife and crosswise cut the orange into thin slices.

	Chewy Oatmeal	Granola	Cinnamon
spice	————	¼ teaspoon ground nutmeg	½ teaspoon ground cinnamon
cereal	2 cups quick-cooking rolled oats	2½ cups granola	2½ cups granola
fruit	————	————	½ cup raisins

ingredients needed for all cookies	2 cups sugar
	¼ cup unsweetened cocoa powder
	½ cup milk
	½ cup butter *or* margarine, cut up
	1 tablespoon light corn syrup
	¼ cup peanut butter

In a 2-quart casserole combine sugar, cocoa powder, and spice (if indicated). Stir in milk. Stir in butter or margarine and corn syrup. Micro-cook, uncovered, on 100% power (HIGH) for 3 to 4 minutes or till mixture is boiling rapidly, stirring once. Micro-cook, uncovered, on 100% power (HIGH) for 3 minutes more, stirring every minute.

Stir in peanut butter, cereal, and fruit (if indicated). Micro-cook, uncovered, on 100% power (HIGH) for 1 to 2 minutes or till mixture is boiling rapidlly. Let stand about 20 minutes. Beat for 3 to 5 minutes or till mixture is slightly thickened. Quickly drop from a rounded teaspoon onto waxed paper. Cool. Makes about 36 cookies.

You should beat the chocolate mixture till it is slightly thickened and just mounds when dropped from a teaspoon.

74

Cherry

2½   cups chow mein noodles

½   cup maraschino cherries, well-drained and halved

Coconut

2   cups quick-cooking rolled oats

¼   cup coconut

Cherry-Orange Spiced Compote (see recipe, page 73) and Chewy Oatmeal No-Bake Cookies

Individual Custards

	Plain	Coffee	Mocha
liquid	1½ cups milk	1½ cups milk	1½ cups milk
flavoring	———	1 tablespoon instant coffee crystals	4 teaspoons presweetened cocoa powder 2 teaspoons instant coffee crystals
garnish	Ground nutmeg	Whipped cream Chocolate curls	Chocolate curls

ingredients needed for all custards	
3	beaten eggs
⅓	cup sugar
¾	teaspoon vanilla
	Dash salt
½	cup hot water

In a 4-cup measure stir together liquid and flavoring (if indicated). Micro-cook, uncovered, on 100% power (HIGH) for 2½ to 3 minutes or till liquid mixture is hot *but not boiling.* Meanwhile, in a mixing bowl combine eggs, sugar, vanilla, and salt. Beat with a wire whisk or rotary beater till well combined. Gradually add hot liquid mixture to egg mixture, mixing well. Divide mixture evenly among four 6-ounce custard cups. Place custard cups in an 8x8x2-inch baking dish. In a 1-cup measure micro-cook hot water, uncovered, on 100% power (HIGH) for 1 to 1½ minutes or till water is boiling. Pour the ½ cup boiling water around the custard cups in the baking dish.

Micro-cook, uncovered, on 100% power (HIGH) for 2½ minutes, rearranging and rotating the custard cups 4 or 5 times. Shake each custard gently to check doneness. Remove any custards that are soft-set (slightly set but not firm). Micro-cook the remaining custards, uncovered, on 100% power (HIGH) for ½ to 1½ minutes more, checking custards for doneness every 10 seconds. Let custards stand 15 to 20 minutes. Serve either warm or chilled and topped with garnish. Makes 4 servings.

Cinnamon	Chocolate	Eggnog
1½ cups milk	1½ cups milk	¾ cup dairy egg nog ¾ cup milk
½ teaspoon ground cinnamon ½ teaspoon finely shredded orange peel	3 tablespoons presweetened cocoa powder	Dash ground nutmeg
Whipped cream	Ground cinnamon	Ground nutmeg

Pour the ½ cup boiling water into the baking dish around the custard cups. The water helps to evenly distribute the microwave energy so that the edges of the custards won't become overcooked before the center is done.

Dollop the coffee custards with whipped cream and top with chocolate curls, if desired.

Gently shake the custards to check for doneness. Remove any that are slightly set but not firm (soft-set). Micro-cook the remaining custards till they are also soft-set.

Orange Cheesecake

	Orange	Black Forest	Apricot-Brandy
liquid	3 tablespoons orange juice	3 tablespoons milk	3 tablespoons apricot brandy
flavoring	1 teaspoon finely shredded orange peel ¼ teaspoon vanilla	2 squares (2 ounces) semisweet chocolate, melted	¼ teaspoon vanilla
topping	¼ cup orange marmalade	¼ cup cherry preserves	¼ cup apricot preserves

ingredients needed for all cheesecakes

3	**tablespoons butter *or* margarine**
⅔	**cup finely crushed graham crackers**
1	**tablespoon sugar**
2	**3-ounce packages cream cheese**
1	**beaten egg**
⅓	**cup sugar**
⅓	**cup dairy sour cream**

For crust, in a 7-inch pie plate micro-cook butter or margarine, uncovered, on 100% power (HIGH) for 45 to 60 seconds or till melted. Stir in crushed graham crackers and 1 tablespoon sugar till all is moistened. Press mixture firmly against bottom and sides of pie plate. Micro-cook, uncovered, on 100% power (HIGH) for 1 to 1½ minutes or till set, rotating pie plate a half-turn after 30 seconds. Set aside.

In a nonmetal mixing bowl micro-cook cream cheese, uncovered, on 50% power (MEDIUM) for 1 to 1½ minutes or till softened. Stir in the beaten egg, ⅓ cup sugar, and sour cream till mixture is smooth. Add liquid and flavoring; mix well. Pour cream cheese mixture into crust. Micro-cook, uncovered, on 50% power (MEDIUM) for 8 to 10 minutes or till a knife inserted 1 inch from edge comes out clean, giving pie plate a quarter-turn every 2 minutes. (Center will be slightly set but not firm.) Cool slightly. Meanwhile, in a small nonmetal bowl or custard cup micro-cook topping on 100% power (HIGH) for 30 to 60 seconds or till warm. Spoon over top of cheesecake. Cool; refrigerate at least 3 hours or till set. Makes 6 servings.

Use your hand to firmly press the crushed graham cracker mixture against the sides and bottom of the pie plate.

The cheesecake should be removed from the microwave oven when a knife inserted 1 inch from the edge comes out clean. The center will not yet be firmly set.

	Apple	Peach	Pear
spice	½ teaspoon ground cinnamon	¼ teaspoon ground nutmeg	¼ teaspoon ground nutmeg Dash ground cloves
fruit	6 medium apples, peeled, cored, and sliced (6 cups)	6 medium peaches, peeled, pitted, and sliced (4 cups)	6 medium pears, peeled, cored, and sliced (4 cups)

ingredients needed for all crisps	
⅓	cup quick-cooking rolled oats
¼	cup packed brown sugar
3	tablespoons all-purpose flour
	Dash salt
3	tablespoons butter *or* margarine
2	tablespoons sugar

In a small mixing bowl combine rolled oats, brown sugar, flour, salt, and spice. Cut in butter or margarine till mixture resembles coarse crumbs; set aside. Place fruit in a 10x6x2-inch baking dish. Sprinkle with sugar. Micro-cook, uncovered, on 100% power (HIGH) for 6 minutes, stirring after 3 minutes. Sprinkle with oat mixture. Micro-cook, uncovered, on 100% power (HIGH) for 3 to 6 minutes or till fruit is tender. Serve warm. Makes 6 servings.

Use a pastry blender to cut the butter or margarine into the rolled oat mixture till the mixture resembles coarse crumbs.

Chiffon Pie

	## Rum	## Amaretto	## Lemon
flavoring	¼ cup light rum	¼ cup Amaretto	¼ cup lemon juice 1 teaspoon finely shredded lemon peel
garnish	¼ cup chopped Brazil nuts	¼ cup sliced almonds, toasted	Lemon twists

ingredients needed for all chiffon pies	
⅓	cup butter *or* margarine
14	graham cracker squares, crushed (1¼ cups)
3	tablespoons sugar
¼	cup sugar
1	envelope unflavored gelatin
¼	teaspoon salt
¾	cup milk
3	beaten egg yolks
3	egg whites
2	tablespoons sugar
½	cup whipping cream

In a 9-inch nonmetal pie plate micro-cook butter or margarine, uncovered, on 100% power (HIGH) for 45 to 60 seconds or till melted. Stir in crushed graham crackers and 3 tablespoons sugar; mix well. Press mixture onto bottom and sides of the pie plate. Micro-cook, uncovered, on 100% power (HIGH) for 2 minutes, rotating dish a half-turn after 1 minute. Cool.

In a large nonmetal mixing bowl combine the ¼ cup sugar, the gelatin, and salt. Stir in milk and egg yolks. Micro-cook, uncovered, on 100% power (HIGH) for 2 to 2½ minutes or till mixture thickens slightly, stirring every 20 to 30 seconds. Cool slightly. Stir in flavoring. Chill to the consistency of corn syrup, stirring occasionally. Remove from refrigerator (gelatin mixture will continue to set).

Using clean beaters beat egg whites till soft peaks form (tips curl over). Gradually add the 2 tablespoons sugar, beating till stiff peaks form (tips stand straight). Whip cream to soft peaks. When the gelatin mixture is the consistency of unbeaten egg whites (partially set), fold the egg whites and the whipped cream into the gelatin mixture. If necessary, chill again till mixture mounds when spooned. Spoon into crust. Chill at least 4 hours or overnight. Top with garnish. Makes 8 servings.

Use a gentle down-up-and-over motion to fold the beaten egg whites and whipped cream into the gelatin mixture.

Cinnamon

flavoring

1	tablespoon sugar
1	teaspoon ground cinnamon
¼	teaspoon ground nutmeg

Sesame Seed

3	tablespoons sesame seed, toasted

Chocolate

2	tablespoons sugar
2	tablespoons unsweetened cocoa powder

ingredients needed for all pie shells

1¼	cups all-purpose flour
¼	teaspoon salt
⅓	cup shortening
1	tablespoon butter *or* margarine
3	to 4 tablespoons cold water

In a mixing bowl stir together flour and salt. Cut in shortening and butter or margarine till mixture resembles coarse crumbs. Stir in flavoring. Sprinkle *1 tablespoon* of the cold water over part of the mixture; gently toss with a fork. Push to side of bowl. Repeat with remaining cold water till all is moistened. Form into a ball. On a lightly floured surface, flatten dough with hands. Roll dough from center to edge, forming a circle about ⅛ inch thick.

Fit pastry into a 9-inch pie plate, being careful not to stretch pastry. Trim pastry ½ inch beyond edge. Fold under and flute edge to form a high rim. Use a fork to prick bottom and sides of pastry at ½-inch intervals. Prick pastry continuously at bend of dish. Micro-cook, uncovered, on 100% power (HIGH) for 5 to 7 minutes or till crust is dry, rotating the dish a quarter-turn twice. Makes one 9-inch pastry shell.

Holding the pastry blender vertically, cut the shortening and butter or margarine into the flour mixture with an down-and-up motion. As necessary between strokes, use a rubber spatula to remove any of the shortening or butter that sticks to the pastry blender.

Pecan

¼ cup finely chopped
   pecans

Cheddar

½ cup shredded cheddar
   cheese (2 ounces)

Sprinkle 1 tablespoon cold water over part of the flour mixture; gently toss with a fork. Push to side of bowl. Repeat this procedure with the remaining water till all the flour mixture is moistened. The dough should be stiff, but not crumbly. If too much water is used, the pastry will be tough and may shrink; if too little is used, it will not hold together.

Use a fork to prick the pastry on the sides, bottom, and continuously at the bend of the dish.

A microwave-cooked pie crust will not appear brown, but will appear dry when it is done.

Glacé Pie

	Peach	Pear	Apricot
spice	¼ teaspoon ground nutmeg	¼ teaspoon ground cinnamon	¼ teaspoon ground allspice
liquid	1½ cups peach nectar	1½ cups pear nectar	1½ cups apricot nectar
fruit	4 cups sliced, peeled peaches *or* one 29-ounce can peach slices, drained and cut up	4 cups sliced, peeled pears *or* one 29-ounce can pear slices, drained and cut up	1 30-ounce can unpeeled apricot halves, drained and cut up

ingredients needed for all pies

½ cup sugar

2 tablespoons cornstarch

½ teaspoon finely shredded orange peel

½ teaspoon vanilla

One-Crust Pie Shell (see recipe, page 82)

Whipped cream

Ground nutmeg, ground cinnamon, *or* ground allspice (optional)

In a 4-cup measure stir together sugar, cornstarch, orange peel, and spice. Add liquid; mix well. Micro-cook, uncovered, on 100% power (HIGH) for 2 to 4 minutes or till mixture is thickened and bubbly, stirring every minute. Micro-cook, uncovered, on 100% power (HIGH) for 2 minutes more, stirring once. Stir in vanilla. Cool slightly (5 to 10 minutes).

Meanwhile, arrange fruit in cooled pastry shell. Pour liquid mixture evenly over fruit. Chill for 2 hours. Dollop with whipped cream. Sprinkle with additional ground nutmeg, cinnamon, or allspice, if desired. Makes 8 servings.

Arrange the fruit in the cooled pastry shell. Then pour the warm liquid mixture evenly over the fruit.

Peach Glacé Pie

Cream Pie

	Vanilla	Coconut	Dark Chocolate
sugar	¾ cup sugar	¾ cup sugar	1 cup sugar
flavoring	————	1 cup flaked coconut	3 squares (3 ounces) unsweetened chocolate, melted

ingredients needed for all cream pies	¼ cup cornstarch
	¼ teaspoon salt
	3 cups milk
	4 beaten egg yolks
	3 tablespoons butter *or* margarine, cut up
	1½ teaspoons vanilla
	One-Crust Pie Shell (see recipe, page 82)
	Whipped cream (optional)

In a large nonmetal mixing bowl stir together cornstarch, salt, and sugar. Gradually stir in milk to make a smooth mixture. Micro-cook, uncovered, on 100% power (HIGH) for 7 to 10 minutes or till mixture starts to boil, stirring every minute. Micro-cook, uncovered, on 100% power (HIGH) for 2 minutes more, stirring every minute.

Gradually stir about *1 cup* of the hot mixture into the beaten egg yolks. Stir yolk mixture into the remaining hot mixture in the mixing bowl. Stir in flavoring (if indicated). Micro-cook, uncovered, on 100% power (HIGH) for 45 to 60 seconds or till just boiling. Stir in butter or margarine and vanilla. Turn into cooled One-Crust Pie Shell. Chill for several hours. Top with whipped cream, if desired. Makes 8 servings.

Stir together the cornstarch, salt, and sugar till the starch particles are separated by sugar. This helps prevent lumps from forming during cooking. Then slowly add the milk, stirring till thoroughly combined.

Pour the hot filling mixture from the bowl into the cooled, micro-cooked pastry shell. Use a wooden spoon or a rubber spatula to guide the mixture into the pastry shell.

Cracker Spread

	Avocado	Herbed	Curry
liquid	½ cup dairy sour cream	2 tablespoons milk	2 tablespoons mayonnaise *or* salad dressing
fruit/ vegetable	1 small avocado, seeded, peeled, and finely chopped	————	2 tablespoons chutney 1 green onion, thinly sliced
seasoning	⅛ teaspoon salt ⅛ teaspoon pepper Few dashes bottled hot pepper sauce Dash garlic powder Dash onion powder	¼ teaspoon dried thyme, crushed ⅛ teaspoon pepper Dash garlic powder	¾ teaspoon curry powder
garnish	Sliced ripe olives	Snipped parsley	Chopped peanuts

ingredients needed for all spreads	½ of an 8-ounce package Neufchâtel cheese
	32 to 40 melba toast rounds *or* shredded wheat crackers

Place Neufchâtel cheese in a nonmetal mixing bowl. Micro-cook, uncovered, on 100% power (HIGH) for 30 seconds or just till softened. Stir together Neufchâtel cheese, liquid, fruit/vegetable (if indicated), and seasoning; mix well. Spread on melba toast rounds or shredded wheat crackers. Arrange 8 appetizers in a circle on a nonmetal plate. Micro-cook, uncovered, on 50% power (MEDIUM) for 45 seconds to 1½ minutes or till heated through, rotating the plate a quarter-turn after 30 seconds. Top with garnish. Serve warm. Repeat with remaining appetizers. Makes 32 to 40 appetizers.

To ensure even heating, arrange the appetizers in a circle. Then rotate the plate a quarter-turn after 30 seconds of micro-cooking.

Cinnamon Cocoa (see recipe, page 91)
and Spicy Snack Mix

Snack Mix

	Traditional	**Spicy**	**Curry**
seasoning	1 tablespoon Worcestershire sauce ½ teaspoon seasoned salt Dash garlic powder	1 teaspoon chili powder ½ teaspoon garlic salt ½ teaspoon bottled hot pepper sauce	½ cup coconut, toasted 2 teaspoons Worcestershire sauce 1 teaspoon curry powder ¼ teaspoon salt
nuts	1 cup peanuts	1 cup mixed nuts	1 cup sunflower nuts

ingredients needed for all mixes	
⅓	cup butter *or* margarine
5	cups desired cereal (cereal options: bite-size shredded corn squares, bite-size shredded wheat squares, bite-size shredded bran squares, bite-size shredded wheat biscuits, round toasted oat cereal, bite-size shredded rice squares, *or* roasted corn snacks)
1	cup chow mein noodles *or* pretzels

Place butter or margarine in a large nonmetal mixing bowl. Micro-cook, uncovered, on 100% power (HIGH) for 1 to 1½ minutes or till butter or margarine is melted. Stir in seasoning. Add desired cereal, chow mein noodles or pretzels, and nuts. Toss gently till all is coated.

Micro-cook, uncovered, on 100% power (HIGH) for 5½ to 6½ minutes or till cereal is toasted, stirring every 2 minutes. Spread in a large shallow pan to cool. Makes about 7 cups.

	Crab	Salmon	Walnut
stuffing	1 5½-ounce can crab meat, drained, flaked, and cartilage removed	1 3¾-ounce can salmon, drained, flaked, and skin and bones removed	¼ cup finely chopped walnuts
seasoning	1 tablespoon finely chopped green pepper 1 teaspoon lemon juice ⅛ teaspoon dried marjoram, crushed	2 tablespoons finely chopped celery 1 teaspoon lemon juice ¼ teaspoon dried dillweed Dash bottled hot pepper sauce	1 teaspoon lemon juice Dash bottled hot pepper sauce
topping	2 tablespoons finely chopped pecans	2 tablespoons sliced almonds, toasted	Pimiento strips

ingredients needed for all stuffed mushrooms	
	12 large fresh mushrooms
	1 3-ounce package cream cheese with chives

Wash and dry mushrooms. Remove stems from mushrooms. Finely chop mushroom stems. In a nonmetal bowl micro-cook cream cheese, uncovered, on 30% power (MEDIUM-LOW) for 1 to 1½ minutes or till softened.

Stir together cream cheese, mushroom stems, stuffing, and seasoning; mix well. Fill *each* mushroom cap with about *1 tablespoon* cream cheese mixture. Top each with some of the topping. Arrange mushrooms in a circle in a 9-inch pie plate. Micro-cook, uncovered, on 100% power (HIGH) for 3 to 4 minutes or till mushrooms are heated through, rotating the dish a half-turn after 2 minutes. Serve warm. Makes 12 appetizers.

Cocoa

	Mint	Cinnamon	Mocha
flavoring	⅓ cup buttermints, crushed	—	3 tablespoons instant coffee crystals
spice	—	1 teaspoon ground cinnamon Dash ground nutmeg	—
garnish	—	Tiny marshmallows (optional)	Chocolate curls (optional)

ingredients needed for all cocoas

2	cups presweetened cocoa powder
1	cup non-dairy creamer
	Sweetened whipped cream (optional)

For beverage mix, stir together cocoa powder, non-dairy creamer, flavoring (if indicated), and spice (if indicated). Store in an airtight container till ready to use.

To make cocoa, place ⅔ cup hot tap *water* in each non-metal cup. Place cup(s) in center of microwave oven. Micro-cook, uncovered, on 100% power (HIGH) till water boils. (Allow 1½ to 1¾ minutes for 1 cup, 2½ to 3 minutes for 2 cups, and 5 to 6 minutes for 4 cups.) Stir ¼ *cup* beverage mix into *each* cup. If desired, top with whipped cream and/or garnish (if indicated). Makes enough mix for 8 servings.

Store the cocoa beverage mix in an airtight container till you are ready to use it.

Garnish the mocha cocoa with whipped cream and chocolate curls, if desired.

	Spicy	*Orange*	*Apple*
juice	⅔ **cup grape juice**	⅔ **cup orange juice**	⅔ **cup apple juice**
spice	4 **inches stick cinnamon, broken** 2 **cardamom pods, opened** 2 **whole cloves**	4 **inches stick cinnamon, broken** 3 **cardamom pods, opened**	3 **cardamom pods, opened** 2 **whole cloves**

ingredients needed for all wines	2 **to 3 tablespoons sugar**
	2½ **cups dry red wine**
	Orange slices

In a 4-cup measure stir together sugar and juice. Tie spice in a cheesecloth bag. Add to juice mixture. Micro-cook, uncovered, on 100% power (HIGH) for 3 minutes. Stir in wine; micro-cook, uncovered, for 2 to 3 minutes more or till hot.

Discard spice bag. Pour wine mixture into 4 mugs. Garnish with orange slices. Makes 4 (6-ounce) servings.

To tie the spice in a cheesecloth bag, place it on a piece of cheesecloth. Bring the cheesecloth up around the spice and tie it closed with a piece of string.

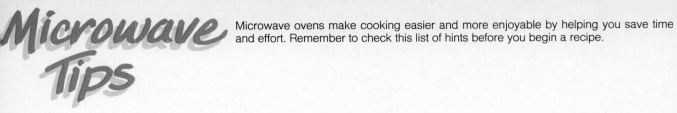

Microwave ovens make cooking easier and more enjoyable by helping you save time and effort. Remember to check this list of hints before you begin a recipe.

warming ice cream toppers
Place the glass jar of ice cream topping in microwave oven. Micro-cook, uncovered, on 100% power (HIGH) till heated through. Allow 45 to 60 seconds for a full 12-ounce jar of topping.

softening unflavored gelatin
Sprinkle unflavored gelatin over the cold liquid specified in the recipe. Let stand for 5 minutes. Micro-cook, uncovered, on 100% power (HIGH) till gelatin is dissolved, stirring once. Allow 45 to 60 seconds for ½ cup liquid; 1½ to 1¾ minutes for 1 cup liquid; and 2 to 2¼ minutes for 1½ cups liquid.

warming breads
Place rolls in napkin-lined basket or on nonmetal plate. Micro-cook on 100% power (HIGH) till warm, turning once. Allow 15 to 20 seconds for one or two rolls, 30 to 50 seconds for 4 rolls, and 40 seconds to 1½ minutes for 6 rolls.

toasting nuts
Spread ¼ cup of desired nuts in a pie plate. Micro-cook, uncovered, on 100% power (HIGH) about 3 minutes or till toasted, stirring frequently.

melting chocolate
Place wrapped chocolate square in microwave oven with folded side of wrapper up. Micro-cook on 100% power (HIGH) till melted. Allow about 2 minutes for one square and 2½ to 3 minutes for two squares. Lift wrappers by folded ends.

making plain croutons
Spread 4 cups of ½-inch bread cubes in a 12x7½x2-inch baking dish. Micro-cook, uncovered, on 100% power (HIGH) for 6 to 7 minutes or till crisp and dry, stirring every 2 minutes.

toasting coconut
Spread ½ cup flaked coconut in a pie plate. Micro-cook, uncovered, on 100% power (HIGH) for 3 to 4 minutes or till golden. After 1½ minutes of micro-cooking, stir coconut every 30 seconds.

softening ice cream
Place 1 quart of solidly frozen ice cream in the microwave oven. Micro-cook on 10% power (LOW) for 40 seconds to 1¼ minutes or till just softened.

plumping raisins, currants, or dried apricots
In a mixing bowl micro-cook 2 cups water, uncovered, on 100% power (HIGH) for 4 to 6 minutes or till boiling. Stir in 1 cup raisins, currants, or dried apricots. Let stand for 5 minutes. Drain off excess water.

thawing frozen whipped dessert topping
Place topping in microwave oven. Micro-cook, uncovered, on 30% power (MEDIUM-LOW) till softened. Allow 45 seconds to 1¼ minutes for a 4-ounce container and 1 to 1¾ minutes for an 8-ounce container.

softening butter or margarine
Place 1 stick of butter or margarine on a nonmetal serving dish. Micro-cook, uncovered, on 10% power (LOW) for 1 to 1½ minutes or till softened.

Index

A-B

Amaretto Chiffon Pie, 81
Appetizers
  Avocado Cracker Spread, 87
  Crab-Stuffed Mushrooms, 90
  Curry Cracker Spread, 87
  Herbed Cracker Spread, 87
  Salmon-Stuffed Mushrooms, 90
  Walnut-Stuffed Mushrooms, 90
Apples
  Apple-Apricot-Spiced Compote, 73
  Apple Brownie Pudding Cake, 71
  Apple Dessert Crisp, 80
  Apple Hot Wine, 92
  Apple-Sauced Turkey, 41
Applesauce Spice Muffins, 64
Apricots
  Apricot-Brandy Cheesecake, 79
  Apricot Glacé Pie, 84
  Apricot Pork Spareribs, 22
  Apricot-Sauced Cornish Hens, 37
  Apricot-Sauced Turkey, 41
  Apricot Scones, 63
  Apricot Swirl Bread, 68
Asparagus Cheese Puff, 47
Avocado Cracker Spread, 87
Bacon
  Bacon-Cheddar Chicken
    Rolls, 40
  Bacon-Cheddar Grits
    Casserole, 61
  Bacon Corn Bread, 66
Banana Spice Muffins, 64
Barbecue-Sauced Meatballs, 30
Barbecue-Style Pork Chops, 16
Barbecue-Style Pork Spareribs, 22
Basil Buttered Fillets, 44
Beef
  Barbecue-Sauced Meatballs, 30
  Beef-Pepper Stir-Fry, 21
  Beef Stew with Dumplings, 14
  Beef Stir-Fry with Vegetables, 18
  Beer-Marinated Beef Roast, 10
  Beer Stew with Dumplings, 14
  Carrot-Stuffed Round Steak, 15
  Cheese-Sauced Round Steak, 17
  Country-Style Pot Roast, 13
  Everyday Meatloaf, 25
  Family-Style Pot Roast, 13
  Garden Stuffed Cabbage Rolls, 26
  Herb-Sauced Round Steak, 17
  Hot Texas Stew with Dumplings, 14
  Italian Pasta Pie, 24
  Italian Stuffed Cabbage Rolls, 26
  Italian-Style Pot Roast, 13
  Mushroom-Stuffed Burgers, 28
  Onion-Stuffed Burgers, 28
  Orange-Glazed Meatloaf, 25
  Oriental Marinated Beef Roast, 10
  Pickle-Stuffed Burgers, 28
  Potato-Stuffed Round Steak, 15
  Sauerbraten-Sauced Meatballs, 30
  Sloppy Joe Meat Sauce, 23
  Spaghetti Meat Sauce, 23

Beef (continued)
  Spicy Beef-Cheese Casserole, 31
  Spinach-Stuffed Round Steak, 15
  Swedish-Sauced Meatballs, 30
  Taco Meat Sauce, 23
  Tomato-Sauced Round Steak, 17
  Wine-Marinated Beef Roast, 10
Beer-Cheddar Cheese Fondue, 50
Beer-Marinated Beef Roast, 10
Beer Stew with Dumplings, 14
Black Forest Cheesecake, 79
Bran Cereal Muffins, 62
Bran-Coated Drumsticks, 38
Bratwurst Macaroni Casserole, 34
Breads
  Applesauce Spice Muffins, 64
  Apricot Scones, 63
  Apricot Swirl Bread, 68
  Bacon Corn Bread, 66
  Banana Spice Muffins, 64
  Bran Cereal Muffins, 62
  Carrot Nut Bread, 67
  Date Scones, 63
  Granola Cereal Muffins, 62
  Ham Corn Bread, 66
  Lemon Swirl Bread, 68
  Nutty Cereal Muffins, 62
  Oatmeal Cereal Muffins, 62
  Orange Swirl Bread, 68
  Pumpkin Nut Bread, 67
  Pumpkin Spice Muffins, 64
  Raisin Scones, 63
  Raisin Swirl Bread, 68
  Rye Yeast Bread, 70
  Sausage Corn Bread, 66
  Spicy Swirl Bread, 68
  Wheat Germ Cereal Muffins, 62
  White Yeast Bread, 70
  Whole Wheat Yeast Bread, 70
  Zucchini Nut Bread, 67
Broccoli Cheese Puff, 47
Broccoli Cheesy Casserole, 57
Brownie Pudding Cake, 71
Buttered Fillets, 44

C-D

California Vegetable Salad, 55
Carrots
  Carrot Cheese Puff, 47
  Carrot Nut Bread, 67
  Carrot-Stuffed Round Steak, 15
  Carrot-Topped Lamb Chops, 19
Cauliflower Cheesy Casserole, 57
Cereal Muffins, 62
Cheese
  Cheddar One-Crust Pie Shell, 82
  Cheddar-Sauced Puffy Omelet, 52
  Cheesecake, 79
  Cheese Casserole, 31
  Cheese Fondue, 50
  Cheese Puff, 47
  Cheese Sauced Round Steak, 17

Cheese (continued)
  Cheese Souffléed Vegetables, 42
  Cheesy Casserole, 57
Cherry Brownie Pudding Cake, 71
Cherry No-Bake Cookies, 74
Cherry-Orange-Spiced Compote, 73
Chewy Oatmeal No-Bake Cookies, 74
Chicken Rolls, 40
Chiffon Pie, 81
Chili-Sauced Pork Roast, 11
Chili-Stuffed Frankfurters, 32
Chocolate Individual Custards, 76
Chocolate One-Crust Pie Shell, 82
Cinnamon Cocoa, 91
Cinnamon Individual Custards, 76
Cinnamon No-Bake Cookies, 74
Cinnamon One-Crust Pie Shell, 82
Coated Drumsticks, 38
Cocoa, 91
Coconut Cream Pie, 86
Coconut No-Bake Cookies, 74
Coffee Individual Custards, 76
Corn-Beer Savory Soup, 54
Corn Bread
  Corn Bread, 66
  Corn Bread-Coated Drumsticks, 38
  Corn Bread-Stuffed Artichokes, 53
  Corn Bread-Stuffed Fish, 46
Country-Style Pot Roast, 13
Country-Style Scrambled Eggs, 49
Country-Style Stuffed Cabbage
  Rolls, 26
Crab-Stuffed Mushrooms, 90
Cracker Spread, 87
Cranberry-Sauced Pork Roast, 11
Cream Pie, 86
Creamy Lamb-Cheese Casserole, 31
Curry
  Curry Cracker Spread, 87
  Curry-Sauced Puffy Omelet, 52
  Curry Snack Mix, 89
Dark Chocolate Cream Pie, 86
Date Scones, 63
Desserts
  Amaretto Chiffon Pie, 81
  Apple Brownie Pudding Cake, 71
  Apple Dessert Crisp, 80
  Apricot-Brandy Cheesecake, 79
  Apricot Glacé Pie, 84
  Black Forest Cheesecake, 79
  Cheddar One-Crust Pie Shell, 82
  Cherry Brownie Pudding Cake, 71
  Chocolate Individual Custards, 76
  Chocolate One-Crust Pie Shell, 82
  Cinnamon Individual Custards, 76
  Cinnamon One-Crust Pie Shell, 82
  Coconut Cream Pie, 86
  Coffee Individual Custards, 76
  Dark Chocolate Cream Pie, 86
  Dessert Crisp, 80
  Eggnog Individual Custards, 76
  Granola Snack Cake, 72
  Lemon Chiffon Pie, 81
  Mocha Individual Custards, 76
  Orange Cheesecake, 79
  Peach Dessert Crisp, 80